GLOBALIZATION AND
SOME OF ITS CONTENTS

GLOBALIZATION AND SOME OF ITS CONTENTS

The Autobiography of a Russian Immigrant

GEORGE ROSEN

To order additional copies of this book, contact:
Xlibris Corporation
1-888-795-4274
www.Xlibris.com
Orders@Xlibris.com
27618

I write in the light of a lamp

The absolute the eternities

Their outlying districts
                    are not my theme

I am hungry for life and for death also

I know what I know and I write it

The embodiment of time
                    the act

The movement in which the whole being

is sculptured and destroyed . . .

                    . . .

I am a history
          a memory inventing itself

I am never alone . . .

I move in the dark
          I plant signs

From: Octavio Paz, "Vindaban," Select Poems (1984), p. 62.

1

Dedication

To the Memory of

My Mother who brought me to America and raised me;

My Uncle Sam and Aunt Sarah who made our coming possible and helped us after we were here; My Aunt Esther and Uncle Isaac who raised me as a boy in Bridgeport and were "Ma" and "Pa" to me;

My Stepfather, Sam Levine, who raised me to be a man.

All died many years ago, and all were Russian immigrants to America, as I am.

And of my generation in my family,

My cousins Walter and Paul who were brothers to me in Bridgeport and ever after, until they died;

My cousin Helen's husband, Sam, who was a brother-in-law to me and one of my closest friends; My nephew John, Walter's son, whose early death in his forties was both a shock and the personal loss of a close friend.

My step-sister Eva, with whom I lived for five years in Brooklyn, and was a close friend thereafter.

My sister-in-law of 25 years, Judy Mitchell, Sylvia's sister, who became my sister as well, whose death just before the end of 2004 was not a surprise but is a great loss for us.

My sister-in-law, Kitt Egan, mother of Kymberlee, my son Mark's wife. Kitt died most unexpectedly as I was writing this book. It is a great shock, and loss, for myself and Sylvia.

And my close friends of over sixty years of my life, many of whom died in the past few years, and who are remembered in this book of my life. One of these very close friends, Martin Blumensons, just died. Three of my closest and longest friends for about 50 years, Terry Neale, Subbiah Kannappan, and Prakash Tandon died while I was writing my book. Their deaths are a great loss.

CONTENTS

INTRODUCTION

I HAD BEEN thinking of writing my autobiography for a few years. I thought I had an interesting life, but I wanted its story to be more than just a chronology of events – it should have a theme. That focus came to me after I read Joseph Stiglitz's *Globalization and its Discontents*. Immigration is an element of globalization. Migrants from all over the world from the 16th century on created the United States and made it what it is today. I am myself one of those immigrants, as was my mother who brought me from Russia when I was three years old, and her brother and sister who were already here and helped us to come. Today there is a strong movement in the United States to restrict immigration and even to close our borders. Even stronger movements are active in many other countries to close their borders to migrants.

I am convinced from my own life and that of many friends of mine that immigration is a very positive part of globalization. I know my life as I have lived it as an American citizen would never have been possible in the Russia I left, and I might not even have lived very long had I remained there. I have had a good life in the United States. Apart from the personal benefits to me and my loved ones, I feel that I've helped to improve the lives of other American citizens, and of people in the many countries in which I have worked. I made Economics my career because

I believed by practicing it I could make that contribution. The greatest economists from Adam Smith to Keynes, including Marx, Marshall and Veblen, stressed that goal of Economics. I hope that my autobiography will continue what I have done in the past by showing not only how I have enjoyed my own life, but have contributed to the well-being of others. By doing so it will strengthen the position of those who support freedom of immigration into the United States and into other countries of the world. That is why I have titled the book *Globalization and Some of its Contents*, as distinguished from "Discontents." In talking with friends who are like myself immigrants to the United States, but from Asia and Latin America as well as Europe, I am struck by their experiences and achievements here compared to what they might have been able to do in their countries of origin. Their hope to achieve this inspired their migration to this country, and our freedom and economic opportunities made it possible. They have also been able to contribute to improved well-being of family members and others in their countries of origin. This contributes to the argument from my own experience.

I am trying my best not to repeat in this autobiography what I have already written in my nine earlier economic research volumes. I've given the titles of those books for any interested reader. This autobiography is of my own life experiences and ideas since I was a child, and not about my economic and social research. I have not kept diaries or journals during my life. I have largely relied on my memory as I've written the manuscript during the summer of 2004, with reference to short published records I have. My memory has become worse with age, and I have forgotten some names and dates. I hope friends will forgive my not mentioning their names and any incorrect dates where they are concerned. The main events are correct.

My wife, Sylvia, has read drafts of those sections of the books where she and her family are involved. Her comments and corrections were essential for the final version. Her memory is much better than mine. Even more important was her support during the many days that I was writing this. It would have been impossible to write without her support.

Geoff Huck, a close friend for many years in Chicago, who now lives in Canada, knows me and my life well. When I first began to think of writing my autobiography he strongly encouraged me to do so, but it took time for me to follow that up until I read Stiglitz's book. I hope this comes up to what he expected, and I thank him very much for his strong encouragement.

The manuscript was written in pencil. Fortunately I have good handwriting and have always done this at an early stage. This penciled version was edited and typed by Susan Gray, a neighbor and friend in Falmouth, who had done the same for my previous book. She has put my handwritten pages into semi final form and improved it in that process for all of which I am most thankful to her.

Final revisions were made by one of my close friends in Chicago, Ann Hoselitz, for which I am very thankful.

CHAPTER I

Growing Up

A. Russian Family Background

I KNOW VERY little of my Russian family history. As I write this I am very sorry that I never asked my mother for more about our family or about my father, but I thought I might hurt her if I did. I also suspect that as part of my Americanization I didn't want to, and it is now too late.

My Russian family was a Jewish family from White Russia, centered about Minsk with its then large Jewish population. My family was a large one generally not well off, but my mother was brought up by a well-to-do uncle living in St. Petersburg, and she was able to study dentistry in that city before 1914. An elder brother, Sam, and sister, Esther, had migrated to the United States from White Russia soon after 1900. Her brother set up a successful photo studio in New York City in the Bronx, settling there and marrying my future Aunt Sarah. Her sister had married a skilled machinist, Isaac Werner, working in Bridgeport, Connecticut. My grandfather and her other brothers and sisters remained in Russia in The White Russia and St. Petersburg regions during this time.

I know that my mother and her family members in Russia were not orthodox Jews, but were secular and non-religious, and were strongly sympathetic to socialism. My mother served as a dentist in the Russian Communist Army after the 1917 Revolution and met my father in that same army in which he was an engineer. I was born in February 1920 in Petrograd, and my father died soon after in the flu epidemic that ravaged Russia in the early 1920's. My mother told me that he had carried me on his shoulders in a parade in Petrograd in which they both marched to hear Trotsky speak. If my father had not died, my mother might have remained in Russia rather than leaving in 1923. I remember nothing about those earliest years of my life. My mother told me I spoke Russian well when we left, but I certainly forgot it soon after coming to the United States. When I tried to learn it about thirty years later, it was very difficult – it had sunk deeper in my subconscious than I expected.

My Uncle Sam in New York thought that my mother would be able to practice dentistry in the United States. He told her that and offered to help bring her with me from Russia if she wished to come. My mother accepted his very kind offer, and she and I left Russia by train for Holland in late 1923, arriving in Rotterdam to find a ship to take us.

B. Coming to the U.S. and Life in Bridgeport

We were able to get steerage passage on the ship *Nieuw Amsterdam* in December and arrived at Ellis Island on December 23rd. On our trip across the Atlantic, I picked up chicken-pox and was interned in the Ellis Island hospital after our arrival. Fortunately, I recovered a few days before the time limit for such internment; if I had not, we would have had to go back to Europe. Uncle Sam met us when I recovered, and we went ashore with him to his and Aunt Sarah's apartment in the Bronx, where we would stay until my mother resettled.

But that resettlement was entirely different from what she and her brother expected. She could not practice dentistry in the U.S. without a New York or other state license. She could not get that without training in dentistry in an American dental school and a degree for that profession – her Russian degree, license and experience were not recognized. She would have to find other work. The only work she could get was in the New York garment trades in the city's sweatshops in short-term, low pay work. She lived in a small flat near the city garment district. She could not care for me nor afford a nurse, so she arranged for me to live with Esther and Isaac in Bridgeport, Connecticut, 50 miles from New York. They had a large house in which space would not be a problem. They had four children ranging from Helen, then age 12, to Gertrude, 2, and including two boys, Walter, 9, and Paul, 4, so that I might grow up with my own generation. Moving to Bridgeport in 1924 gave me 4 sisters and brothers – relatives called cousin-sisters and cousin-brothers in India's extended family system. Living with my cousin-brothers and sisters for 8 years was undoubtedly the most important formative experience in my life. I learned English quickly – the children did not know Russian of course, and I had to speak English to play and talk with them.

We were a Jewish family, but a secular one. My uncle and aunt were members of the Workmen's Circle. This was an organization, the *Arbeiter Ring*, that was started in East Europe by Jews of a socialist orientation. The Jewish migrants to the United States from East Europe established the American equivalent with the same name in English. There was a very active branch in Bridgeport, an industrial city with many migrants. This Bridgeport branch set up a Jewish school to teach Yiddish, and Jewish history based on the Old Testament, to Jewish children. There were many family events and meetings of Jewish adults to exchange ideas, to celebrate Jewish holidays in a secular fashion and to advocate social causes.

With Bridgeport being a major industrial city in Connecticut and near New York a large number of workers from many European countries other than Russia lived there. These workers, from Hungary, the Balkans and Italy among other countries, had socialist traditions, and it was not surprising that Bridgeport had one of the largest socialist parties in the United States. During the 1930's Depression, Bridgeport elected a Socialist mayor, Jasper McLevy, and was the only city other than Milwaukee, Wisconsin to have a Socialist Party mayor.

My cousins and I attended the Bridgeport public schools. I only went to grammar school, since I moved to Brooklyn after finishing eighth grade; my cousins completed high school. We got good educations in basic reading, writing and arithmetic and also literature and history. The city's public library was excellent with a great variety of books from the classics to the nineteenth and early twentieth century novelists, and we read them. I myself read and saw some Shakespeare, and read Dickens, Conrad and Hemingway before I left Bridgeport.

When I was about seven years old, we moved to North Bridgeport on Capitol Avenue, and I lived there until I was twelve. I visited that address this summer with Gertrude, my cousin two years younger than I am, who also lived there then and after I left Bridgeport for Brooklyn. She recalls that we were living in near poverty, but I certainly didn't think that then. Paul and I shared a room, and Gert remembers hearing both of us arguing and yelling about sports – we were baseball and basketball fans. In the backyard there was a basketball net into which we would throw balls, and several small golf holes into which we played miniature golf. Walter caddied at the local club. The public grammar school and the Jewish school we went to weekly were within easy walking distance, and schoolmates lived nearby, some on the same street. Gert remembers how unhappy I was to leave there when I did in 1932.

At home we read the "Jewish Forward" with its socialist approach in Yiddish, and also got and read the "Bridgeport Post" daily, and the "New York Times" on weekends. This socialist, secular education and approach to life was a fundamental basis for my attitudes and the framework of my thinking on social policy issues, especially during and after the 1930's Depression, and it contributed greatly to my decision to go into Economics as the field of my career.

My elder cousins' aims and experiences after grammar school influenced mine after I left Bridgeport. My aunt and uncle made it possible for them to achieve those aims. Helen, my oldest cousin, wanted to go to college after she finished high school in about 1930. This was very unusual for a Jewish girl at that time. Her mother strongly supported her wish and her father's work made it possible. She went to college in Bridgeport and then to New York University for graduate work. Her brother Walter was an excellent high school student and was admitted to Yale in about 1932 as an undergraduate, which was then rare for a Jewish applicant. Walter majored in Economics as an undergraduate, did well and went on to Yale Law School, where he edited the Law Journal. Paul, one year older than I, was also admitted to Yale as an undergraduate majoring in science before going into the Air Force when the U.S. entered World War II. Gert later followed Helen into college and her own career. The fact that all my cousins went to college and beyond influenced my own plans and intentions. Walter's majoring in Economics and his study with Thurman Arnold and Walton Hamilton, two leading institutional economists, was a factor in my decision to go into that field.

One of my greatest pleasures in Bridgeport was the summer and our daily swimming. Bridgeport is on Long Island Sound and has a lovely beach, Seaside Park, on the Sound. During the summer, my Uncle would drive my Aunt and the children who were at home to the beach every morning on his way to the factory where he worked. He left us off and then picked us up on the way home after his work day ended, and he went for his swim. It was a great pleasure and made my taste for salt-water ocean swimming when I grew up, rather than fresh water and swimming pools.

I had eight great and formative years with my Aunt and Uncle and cousins in Bridgeport from 1924-1932. During that time, I saw my mother about once a month when she came for the weekend or holiday in Bridgeport – we went down to New York sometimes on family visits. My mother, on her days off from work, was active in the International Ladies Garment Workers Union (The ILGWU) and politically as a socialist. She also enjoyed theatre, ballet and concerts in the city. In 1931 she married Sam Levine, a widower and older man, who owned a stationery store in the Flatbush section of Brooklyn. He had come to the U.S. from Russia before 1914, first to the Midwest where he had been a farmer, as his Russian family had been, before he moved to New York to open his store.

He had five children by his first marriage. Those children were adults when he married my mother. The two sons had their own careers and homes: Max, a dentist, was married and with a family living and working in the New York area, and Morris, partnering with his father in the Brooklyn store, was married and living with family near the store. Two of the three daughters, Jeanette and Ida, were married with their husbands, Harry and Sigmund, successful businessmen, living in Brooklyn with their children. The third and youngest daughter, Eva, lived with her father and my mother in Brooklyn, and worked in New York. She was about ten years older than I was.

C. Living in Brooklyn and High School and College

The apartment of my stepfather and mother was near the store in Flatbush, and that is where I went to live. It was also within walking distance of Erasmus Hall High School, the oldest public school in New York city, going back to the Dutch settlement. I began going to Erasmus Hall in September 1932. It was an excellent school that gave me a very good education. I had excellent classes in Latin and English. I am told it is not as good today as it was then. I still remember, almost 70 years after I graduated, the names of my English teacher, Ms. Molendyk and my Latin teacher, Ms. Burns, who taught me literature and writing and Latin in a straightforward and effective manner, and whose benefits I still have. (Erasmus then also had one of the best school football teams in the city with Sid Luckman the quarterback.)

After my day in school, I worked in the store, waiting on customers, placing papers and magazines on display, and making myself generally useful. At that time there were many newspapers in New York – more than today – with different viewpoints, and I enjoyed reading them. We also sold cigarettes and cigars, and we had several pin-ball machines before they became illegal. Watching the players of those machines turned me off from gambling as an adult.

I was not very close to my mother and stepfather. We very much loved each other, and they were very helpful if I came to them with an obvious wish, but I did not confide to them about my personal desires or any problems I might have. With their very different experiences and backgrounds I did not feel they would understand what I might want. I decided what I wanted and told them, and if I needed help asked them without any discussion. They usually gave me what I wanted since I realized what we could afford. My relations with my step-brothers and sisters were cordial, but not close, except for Eva, with whom I lived for some years. Eva was a good friend, but older than I was with her own life, and she married a few years after I arrived. She and her husband, Harry, remained good friends, as their son, Arthur, was later. Three of my stepfather's children lived in or near Brooklyn, and we saw each other quite often. They were much older than I was, and their children were several years younger, so there was little emotional exchange among us. I have been in touch with a few of their children as an adult, but am in close contact with only one. She is my stepniece, Gladys, who married my cousin Paul during the Second World War, after my mother put them in touch with each other. She became a sister to me in the same sense as Paul, while alive, was a brother.

As in Bridgeport, I was in a secular family. My mother and stepfather were not religious. In Brooklyn I no longer went to a Jewish school since there was none near where I lived, and we did not attend religious services. I was not bar mitzvahed when I reached 13; neither Walter nor Paul had been bar mitzvahed in Bridgeport. My parents and I had good Christian, as well as Jewish friends, in our neighborhood and in high school.

New York in the 1930's was a very stimulating city with movies, concerts, plays and museums within easy reach from my home in Flatbush. The subways were safe, and I could take them by myself to get to where I wanted to go. Politically, that decade was one of the city's greatest. Fiorello LaGuardia was a very liberal city mayor, Herbert Lehman was Governor of the state, and the President of the U.S. was the former state governor, Franklin D. Roosevelt, America's greatest President during my life. The Socialist Party, headed by Norman Thomas, was very active, and there was a strong socialist-communist intellectual movement centering around "The Partisan Review" journal and intellectuals at CCNY and Columbia University. It was a stimulating environment to grow up in – my mother participated in it, and she encouraged me to do so during high school and college after school and work.

I graduated from Erasmus Hall in 1936 and went on to Brooklyn College, part of New York City's free City College system that provided a high quality education to qualified students who might not be able to afford private college or might not be admitted into many with their quotas for Jewish and other minorities. In my first year of college, the Brooklyn College campus was quite a distance from my home, taking about an hour each way by subway or bus. But from the second year on, a new campus had been built and was open, and that was about a ten minute walk from where I lived. The College President was then Harry Gideonse, a major economist from the University of Chicago, and the faculty included many distinguished scholars.

At that time Brooklyn College had a large number of Jewish students. This reflected their families' wish to send their children to college so that they might have better jobs than in the sweatshops and small retail/ wholesale shops and stores where the children's parents worked. The East European Jews had not reached the incomes, living standards and status of the German Jews who had migrated to the U.S. after 1848 and succeeded. Herbert Lehman had been elected Governor of New York and Robert Morgenthau was Treasury Secretary in Franklin Roosevelt's Cabinet. During the Depression, private college tuition was high in real terms, and admission was often limited so that Brooklyn College offered a real alternative toward the desired family goal. (Today the country's public colleges and universities, including various city colleges, offer a similar opportunity to lower income Black, Latin and Asian students with similar goals.)

When I began college, I had not decided in what subject to major. I very much enjoyed reading literature and while in Erasmus had read in class or on my own many of the great writers. These included Homer, Caesar and Cicero in English classes, English authors from Shakespeare to Dickens, Conrad and Joyce, and major American writers, including Hemingway, Fitzgerald and Faulkner, English translations of such Russian writers as Tolstoy and Dostoevsky and French authors including Balzac and Proust. I read these for pleasure rather than for career purposes. I hoped that I would contribute to making a better world in some way after I finished schooling.

I took some courses in Economics at Brooklyn and decided to major in Economics. The Great Depression had not ended in 1936 when I began college, and with my Uncle Isaac's factory work and my mother's sweatshop labor I was especially interested in problems of unemployment, conditions of labor and the role of trade unions. These interests of course also reflected my socialist upbringing in Bridgeport. Theresa Wolfson, who was one of the early women economists, taught Labor Economics at Brooklyn. She was a great teacher with a deep interest in her students, and she had a great influence on me and my classmates.

The Brooklyn College Economics Department was not a department that taught competitive market theory. Most of the faculty were institutional economists, followers of Thorstein Veblen, and with degrees from Columbia where they had studied with Wesley Clair Mitchell and J.M. Clark, leading contemporary institutional economists who had influenced Franklin Roosevelt's New Deal economic policies. The faculty were also influenced by socialist thought and knew Marx's work; none were Communists. In our Economics courses we did not start with Neo-Classical Competitive Market Theory, and I did not study that subject as an undergraduate. There were strong courses in the History of Economic Thought, including the work of the Mercantilists, Adam Smith, Ricardo, Marx and some Marshall; there were also courses on Thorstein Veblen and John R. Commons and Institutional thought. I read these institutional economists then, as well as Thurman Arnold and Walton Hamilton, with whom Walter had studied at Yale. These economists stressed the interaction of economics with the broader social system and the value of economics as a tool for both understanding society and improving its functioning so as to make possible a better life for all the people in this country and the wider world. Socialism and Communism were seen as economic systems trying to create paths to a better world also, and deserved study as such.

I also took stimulating courses in the English Department, which had excellent teachers in Literature, and in the History Department, in which some of the faculty were German refugee professors who had fled from Hitler. These made us aware of Fascism and what was then going on in Europe. Apart from my classes, it was in college that I began reading Edmund Wilson, then a socialist, and in my opinion one of the leading American literary and social critics, and the wider group of "Partisan Review" authors, whom in general I found very stimulating and enjoyable both as artists and critics.

Between my college studies and my work in the store after school, I did not have much time to take part in campus activities, including political ones. At that time, too, I was still below 21, the then starting voting age. However, I had a strong political interest and supported both the New Deal and Norman Thomas' socialist ideas at meetings I might go to every so often. In international affairs I strongly supported the Spanish Republic after 1936 when Franco's Revolution and Civil War began. If I had been older, I might well have volunteered for the Abraham Lincoln Brigade in support of the Spanish Government, but I could not then. I was strongly opposed to Fascism both in Italy under Mussolini with his attack on Ethiopia and in Germany with Hitler's takeover of Austria and Czechoslovakia. I of course knew of Nazi anti-Semitism, but had no sense of its extremes and what it would become. At that time, while I was not an isolationist or an appeaser in my thinking, I was against American military alliance with England and France against Hitler. After Hitler's Czech takeover in early 1939, I felt stronger steps should be taken against him, and I was prepared to join the then strongly anti-Nazi, Communist led American Student Union on campus in the Fall 1939 term. But after Stalin signed his treaty with Hitler in mid-1939, I no longer thought of joining the ASU. That treaty contributed directly to Hitler's attack on Poland in September 1939 with Russia supporting the attack and sharing in the land conquests. I supported the English and French declarations of war against the Nazis, but I did not then think the United States should enter a European War after the recent experience of the First World War.

Brooklyn College then had a student body with a large Jewish component, and I knew few non-Jewish students. My friends were almost all fellow students and Economics majors. Several with whom I went to graduate school remained friends for life, but I have lost touch with all the others. Almost all stayed in Economics or related fields, some with government agencies, others in business, journalism and non-profits, and several in academic careers, but I assume all have retired by now, and I know some have died.

I graduated in June 1940 standing high in my class. I decided I wanted to do graduate work in Economics. I applied to several major schools in and near New York, including Princeton. Theresa Wolfson's help was crucial in gaining admission to Princeton. Princeton, with Douglas Brown and David McCabe on its faculty, was very strong in Labor Economics; the Institute for Advanced Study (IAS) at Princeton had several senior economists who had been at the Brookings Institute when Theresa Wolfson studied there, and all thought highly of her. In the Spring of 1940 she drove down to Princeton with me and two fellow students, Arnold Sametz and Sidney Sheiner, to introduce us to those faculty members and IAS scholars and to recommend us for admission to the Graduate School. We were admitted, Arnold and I accepted and went to Princeton; Sidney chose Harvard Business School. Princeton's Graduate School was then far more open to Jewish students than the College; (Richard Feynman was also a student there then, among others.) Tuition was only $200 per year, significantly below Princeton undergraduate tuition. Total enrollment in the Graduate College was about 200 students, and the number in the Economics Department was about 15. This was small enough so that we would know the faculty quite closely and we would know each other – both of these were major advantages and unusually so in hindsight. (Another Brooklyn College graduate, Alvin Karchere, entered Princeton Graduate School the next year.)

My parents could not afford the Princeton tuition in lump sum at that time. My Uncle Sam, who had made my migration to the U.S. possible 17 years earlier, provided that $200 for the first year, and I started there in September 1940.

C. Princeton Graduate College and Before the Army

Princeton was a very broadening experience for me socially as well as for my education, and it was the basis for my later career throughout the world. It was a gateway to a life I would never have had if I had remained in Russia or Europe. I also think that the experience I then got as a graduate student at Princeton would be difficult, if not impossible, to get in today's academia.

A major cause of that uniqueness was the small student body which made close contact among students, and with faculty, possible. Most of the students had rooms in the Graduate College Dormitory, and we all ate together in the Dining Commons. In my first year I could not get a room in the Dorm, but I ate there. I lived in a house on Mercer Street within easy walking distance of the College. Another graduate student, Bob Ottman, an English major, had the other room in the same house that first year, and we became good friends. Living on Mercer Street I was not far from Albert Einstein's home, and I would often see him walking there, though I was sorry we never met. In my second year, 1941-1942, I had a fellowship which covered the tuition and a room in the Graduate College where I then lived.

All of the Economics graduate students knew each other and became friends. We were not competitors – we exchanged ideas both in and out of classes. The classes were small, often with as few as 5 students to a class and no larger than 10 students. Out of class we often ate together and with other social scientists, as well as others; we then discussed broader, non-academic subjects, as well as Economics. We socialized together in town and sometimes went to New York with friends to do something there.

I of course knew Arnold Sametz and Al Karchere from College, but I made new friends from all over the United States and of different social and religious backgrounds. Ansley Coale, Lionel McKenzie, Don Curtis, Randall Hinshaw, Dillon Glendinning, among others were all Economics graduate students at the time. They opened up other parts of the country for me: Ansley from Maryland, Lionel from Georgia, Don from Maine and Dillon and Randall from California. Don especially influenced my thinking further toward an institutional, policy-oriented approach. He had studied with Kenneth Galbraith who had been on the Princeton faculty for several years before 1940. Galbraith's institutional, policy-oriented approach to Economics had a strong effect upon Don's economic thinking, and Don and I often exchanged ideas on the appropriate character of Economics.

Apart from Economics students, I also knew some students in other departments – Bob Ottman in English, Milton Esman in Politics and Richard Feynman in Physics among others. Except for Bob I didn't know them as well as my Economics classmates, but they were intellectually stimulating. An obvious absence at the time was that Princeton, like other all male universities then, had no female faculty, nor did it admit female students. Some of the male students were married, and I met their wives – Sue Coale and Frankie Hutner – whom I enjoyed, but there was little chance to gain a female perspective on economic issues. I have been struck by today's contrast; then I would never have predicted that Princeton would have had a Jewish president, as it had until recently, or a female president, as it has now. There are also today many faculty and students of both sexes and various religions and ethnic backgrounds. This change can only be positive for both educational and social reasons.

But my impressions of the graduate schools with which I have interacted in more recent years, as well as my experience after returning to academic life in 1972, is that the interchange with my fellow students that I had at Princeton is no longer common. Rather, there is strong competition among the students in one's field, and many feel that if they exchange ideas their ideas may be stolen in some way or other. There is also very little contact with students in other disciplines, given the pressure of time and space and thus little broadening of serious interests beyond one's own field. This has contributed to narrowing the scope of Economics and its usefulness for understanding and dealing with broader policy issues at home and abroad.

The Economics Faculty at Princeton was excellent, and the small class size made it possible for the students to have personal contact and exchange of ideas with their teachers in fields of interest. When I entered Princeton, Labor Economics was my main interest, and I took classes with Professors Brown and McCabe. I also took classes in Neo-Classical Economic Theory for the first time. The teachers of these classes were Professor McIsaac at the introductory level and more significantly

Professors Oskar Morgenstern and Friedrich Lutz at advanced levels. They had come from Austria and Germany to Princeton and were major theorists. I studied Micro-Theory from Jevons to Marshall that I had not read before, and the Austrian economists – Wieser, Böhm-Bawerk, von Mises and Schumpeter. All of these stressed the policy relevance of Economics analysis. Schumpeter in particular emphasized the dynamic character of the economy, the key role of the business cycle in that dynamism, which is driven by technological change, and this is so important today. When I returned to Princeton in 1945-1946, I attended Professor Morgenstern's course on the book that he and von Neumann had just written, *The Theory of Games and Economic Behavior*, which is very important in Economics today, although it has had little effect upon my own work. My key intellectual stimulus among Princeton's faculty was Professor Frank D. Graham who taught courses in International Trade and Monetary Economics. In International Trade we started with Ricardo's Theory of Comparative Advantage progressing through John Stuart Mill's ideas and the work of Frank Taussig and Graham's own work. In the Money Course we studied the Quantity Theory of Money, alternative monetary standards and John Maynard Keynes' ideas culminating in his General Theory and the founding of today's Macro Economics. Frank Graham had the fundamental belief that Economics should be used for public policy purposes to make possible the better functioning of the economy for achieving a better society: one that provided employment for all its people and a high quality of life in terms of availability of goods and services for them. The purpose of Economics was not to forecast business prospects or financial values; it was to influence and advise on public policy. It was truly Political Economy in the great British tradition. In the summer of 1941 I read all of Keynes' *General Theory*. That book opened my eyes to the public policy use of Economics in a way that no other book had, and I believe it provides the best policy framework for dealing with the downturns of the business cycle. Unfortunately, I have a sense that Keynes' ideas are largely forgotten today by American economists and policy makers facing the current economic slowdown. Keynes also wrote well for a wide public – a rare skill of today's economists. Graham was also strongly influenced by Veblen's institutional approach, and realized that the economy was one part of a larger social and political system that ultimately determined both the economy's functioning and the scope of economic policy change.

In addition to those courses, I also took courses in related Money and Banking subjects with Professors Edwin Kemmerer and Harley Lutz, both more conservative and orthodox in their approaches to monetary and fiscal policy than Professor Graham. Professor Kemmerer, after the First World War, had been one of the first American economic advisers to foreign countries, including some now termed "less developed" to deal with their economic problems. He was a pioneer for many economists working in the IMF and World Bank, after the Second World War.

While I took courses in Labor Economics with Professors Brown and McCabe and found those personally interesting and stimulating, I found them less so than the broader Trade and Macro-Economic courses with Professor Graham and decided I would do my doctoral work in one of those fields. However, one of the great benefits from my interest in the Labor Economic field was that Professor McCabe arranged, through a friend of his in the Steel Workers Union in Pittsburgh, for me to work as an unskilled worker in a metal-working plant in McKees Rocks, Pennsylvania, not far from Pittsburgh, for $15 per week in the summer of 1941.

This was the first time I had worked in a factory and the first time I had lived away from home or school and beyond a 50 mile radius from Bridgeport or New York. The experience not only gave me a knowledge of how a factory worked, but also a sense of independence and a belief in my own ability to live in a new environment. I had no problem working in the factory, and I met some of its workers. I lived with a worker's family in town, ate in the local cafeteria, went to a movie about once a week, and on the weekend went into Pittsburgh for a good meal. (I could do this on my pay then.) My landlord's family was friendly, and I talked with him or his wife several times during the week. They were Catholic, their parents from an East European country. I remember they had never met a Jew before. They were interested in my background and religion, and they were struck by the fact I did not go to any church – but I, of course, never had with my very secular upbringing. That family could not have been friendlier, and my living with them introduced me for the first time to a Catholic family and introduced them to a real Jewish person. On most evenings during the week I read Keynes' *General Theory* or an Economics book in French or German in my room in preparation for my Ph.D. language exams. (Math was not a requirement in contrast to today.)

I came back to Princeton for the Fall 1941 semester with my Fellowship for 1941-1942, this time living in the Graduate College, and in somewhat closer contact with other students. As in my first year, several times each month I would go into Brooklyn, hitchhiking a ride there, to see my parents, help in the store, and possibly see a play, movie or concert in the city. I did not talk much about my Princeton classes with my parents since what I was taking meant little to them, but we wanted to see each other. At that time, too, I had no girlfriends in New York or elsewhere and that was no reason for going to the city. My interest in dating and sex was late. Among Jewish families then these activities were related to marriage or marriage plans, and I had no such intentions. Several of my friends at Princeton did have girl friends with whom they were in contact, but that didn't affect me. At Princeton, too, I first heard of homosexuality supposedly among some graduate students. This was for me an entirely new type of sexual behavior and of little interest.

In the political field I had strongly supported Franklin Roosevelt's reelection for a third term in 1940, although I had been unable to vote. I favored the New Deal economic policies and social polices, such as the introduction of Social Security and the Wagner Act with respect to collective bargaining and trade union recognition. In the international field I favored non-military aid to England and France after war began in 1939, but was still against military support, and after France collapsed in 1940, I favored military aid to England. I remember asking Douglas Brown, who had fought in the First World War if he had been sorry for that, and he replied that he still thought he had done the right thing, and that supported my view in favor of helping England. In summer 1941 Hitler invaded Russia despite his 1939 treaty with Russia, and if that were successful it would endanger England even more and potentially the U.S. My mother told me later in 1941 that she had a letter from a

Russian relative, for the first time in many years. In that letter she was told that her father, my grandfather, had been killed by the Nazis in White Russia.

On December 7th the issue of American involvement in the war was resolved. Japan attacked Pearl Harbor that morning. I heard that while eating lunch in the Graduate College. I remember the surprise and the shock when my classmates and I heard the news of the attack and the extent of the damage. The United States was at war with Japan and a few days later with German and Italy. My friends would soon become active fighters. Most of us were able to complete that academic year in June 1942 and get our M. A. degrees. We then left Princeton for the Army or Navy or some defense related work.

I myself had registered for the draft at the required date, but because of my poor eyesight and glasses I was not called up immediately. I was to be called up in early December 1942. In the five months between June and my prospective call-up, I worked as an economist in the Office of Price Administration in Washington, D.C. My work was in the "Other Rubber Products" Division (other than "Tires and Tubes," thus including condoms) headed by Everett Hawkins. Hawkins was a recent Princeton Economics Ph.D. who had been a student of Frank Graham and Douglas Brown and a contemporary of Ken Galbraith, the OPA Director. The "Other Rubber Products Division" set prices for rubber products under its control. I learned about the companies making those products and their costs of production, in the process meeting with officers from those firms as well as from other firms whose prices were set by OPA. My association with business officers at that level was a new experience for me, and one that would be valuable for my later post-war work.

This OPA job was the first time I had ever been in Washington, D.C. At that date it was a small town compared to New York City, though it was the capitol of the country. I lived in a small apartment on upper Connecticut Avenue, and the office where I worked was in a temporary building recently constructed near the recently opened National Gallery of Art. I could get to my office by bus in fairly short time; at lunch I could go to the Gallery café, get a bite and browse briefly in one of the galleries looking at the art before returning to work. In the evening my favorite memory is of going to live concerts at the Library of Congress. The ones I best remember are those of the Budapest Quartet, which had recently come to the U.S. from Europe. Those concerts introduced me to Chamber Music – a pleasure that has truly lasted. One of the works I heard first played at those concerts was Mozart's "G Minor Quintet," which I think is one of his greatest and most powerful compositions, and I cannot hear it often enough since.

While I was in Washington, I decided I should go into the Army and actively fight against the Nazis. My cousin Paul, who had graduated from Yale, was serving in the U.S. Air Force in Australia fighting against the Japanese. Close friends and fellow students were in the Navy serving in the Pacific and Atlantic Oceans. I decided I would enlist in an active part of the Army. I did not want to be drafted and assigned to an office post in the army because of my eye problems and university and OPA experience. I therefore enlisted in the Signal Corps to do active work in the army ground forces, and began military service in December 1942.

CHAPTER II

"You're In the Army Now"

M Y FIRST SIX months in the Signal Corps were at Fort Edison in New Jersey where I had basic training. Essentially basic training was preparation for a soldier's life. It included body buildup by hiking, running, and obstacle climbing. There was training in discipline: learning to take orders with no questions asked by such controls as bed checks on dirt on or under beds, KP duty in kitchen serving officers meals and cleaning up after they ate, and guard duty of a day and night at posts around the camp. Direct military training was an essential part of the training. We learned how to fire weapons and took a shooting test and after the test were given a carbine which we wore on our hikes and marches. Most of this basic training was in new activities which I had never done before, but for many of my fellow troops who came from rural backgrounds shooting and cross-country hiking had been part of their normal activities.

After we finished basic training, we began our radio repair training. First we studied about radios, passing a test. Then we began actual work on radios, learning both their proper functioning in and out of vehicles and how to repair them. One of the reasons I had selected the Signal Corps for service was to learn if I had any mechanical ability. I had never done any mechanical work before joining the Army. As part of our training, we were sent to the Philco Radio factory in Philadelphia for several months to learn how the mobile vehicle radios were built and to actually practice the building and repair of the radios in the factory. This was useful training, and I also enjoyed living in Philadelphia for the first time in my life.

Since Camp Edison and Philadelphia were not far from New York, I was able to get back every so often to see family and to see some plays on Broadway, and also to visit Bridgeport. The most important personal family event was the death of my Uncle Sam from cancer in early 1943. He had played such an important role in my life by his help for my mother's immigration to the United States, with me along, and most recently for my first year at Princeton. Unfortunately, I could not get leave to attend his funeral since an uncle was not considered a sufficiently close relative by the Army to grant a leave for his funeral.

I was on friendly terms with the other men in my training company though they were from different social groups than the people I knew before December 1942. Few, if any, were intellectuals or Jewish. Most came from farm families and had been brought up with machines, tools and motor vehicles and knew how to use, drive and repair them. I had none of those skills. Most were also bigger and stronger than I was and had more physical experience than I did. But we got along well, and I had no sense of being picked on or excluded in any way because of my different background.

After my basic and technical training, I was assigned to the 187th Signal Repair Company as a radio repairman with the rank of Corporal. The Company was divided into platoons of about 25 men each under the command of a Lieutenant. Each platoon was to be assigned to an armored division to maintain and repair that unit's tank and other vehicle radios. I was with the 187th Signal Repair Company for my entire Army service and worked in the same platoon as well.

In the Fall of 1943 the Company was sent to the Desert Training Center in Indio, California – the southern desert part of the state – for field training before we would sail to the Pacific Theater. We traveled by train across the country, stopping briefly in Chicago to change trains, enroute to Seattle, from where we would take another train to Los Angeles and Indio eventually. This was my first trip across the United States and to any of those cities. Thirty years later I would move to Chicago for much of my career, but on that first few hours' visit I remember eating a lunch at Berghoff's Restaurant, with one of my fellow soldiers who knew and liked it from one of his earlier civilian visits to Chicago. Montana was an especially beautiful landscape on that train trip, and I remember that we could see Mr. Rainier from the camp where we stayed near Seattle for a few days before we went south.

The Desert Training Center itself in November 1943 was very hot in the daytime and very cold at night. We did some mobile maneuvers in our training there and then learned that the company orders had been changed. Instead of going to the Pacific we were now assigned to Europe, and we would leave for Great Britain from the east coast in early 1944. In early December we got on a troop train for New York, this time traveling by a southern route from Los Angeles to New Orleans, then north to Chicago along the Mississippi and then to New York. Then we had home leave until we would meet again to leave by sea for Europe. I was very glad to be with my parents and relatives in Brooklyn, and I also went to Bridgeport for a few days to visit family there. However, near the end of my home leave I became ill with flu and had to go to the Governor's Island Military Hospital for a week. I fortunately recovered in time to rejoin the 187th Company before it sailed for Europe in late January. If I had not recovered in time, I would have been reassigned to some other entirely different unit.

The 187th left Boston for England on a small ship, probably a freighter, in a large convoy of troop ships protected by destroyers. The enlisted men were berthed in the steerage. The weather in late January was wintry, cold with rough seas, and it was a long trip. I was lucky in that unlike many of the other troops I did not get seasick and was able to move about on deck while others had to stay in bed. (I have been on other cross-ocean trips since then and have not gotten seasick on those. It may be due to my genes – not from anything I have done.) Eventually we landed in Liverpool and from there took a short boat trip to Belfast arriving in early February. We were stationed in a camp outside of Belfast for several months. A pleasant surprise on my arrival there was the news that my cousin Helen in Bridgeport had just given birth to a second child, her and Sam's son Andrew.

In North Ireland we continued our training moving about by foot and by trucks, camping for extended periods, shooting weapons, and of course doing radio repair in armored vehicles. There were also the regular camp duties – guard and KP. Guard duty was considered of particular importance because the IRA was presumed to be strong in Belfast. I remember that on the evening of St. Patrick's Day I was on special guard duty because of a suspected threat.

Apart from military duty I and other soldiers went into Belfast at times for a meal or a movie in the evening or an weekends. The city was blacked out at night, but some places were open. I had also met a young Irish woman who was pleasant company and a very good guide to the city. Near Belfast there was attractive rural and hill country and several old castle sites which I very much enjoyed visiting on weekends. I would have liked to visit Dublin, but the Irish Free State was not in the war and we were not permitted to go there.

In April, the 187th moved to England to join the Third Army there. We were based in Banbury, and the platoons were attached to the different armored divisions of that army to do radio repair work. We did such repair work for the division to which we were assigned, and we also received further mobile warfare training. As part of that mobile training, my platoon went by truck to Wales and South England for several days to practice moving from one place to the other and overnight camping. We became accustomed to moving and to working on the move; this was good training for what we would in fact do later in France and Germany. A pleasant by-product of this training travel was that I saw the beautiful Welsh country – one of the U.K.'s loveliest regions.

We were restricted in our personal travels from Banbury to a radius of 25 miles from that city. Oxford and Stratford were within that limit, and I visited both for the first time; London was too far out and I could not go there. In and around Banbury we could also see stark evidence of the destruction caused by German air bombing attacks.

On June 7th, D-Day, we were not on or near the English Channel, but we saw and could hear overhead the fleets of attacking planes associated with the Allied landings in France. Soon after D-Day, we, as part of the Third Army, left Banbury for the English Channel coast. After we reached there, we were soon restricted to camp and began preparations to cross the English Channel as part of Patton's Third Army. My platoon crossed by ship on the night of July 13th, landing on the 14th, Bastille Day, on Utah Beach with trucks and repair equipment. The landing was peaceful since the Utah Beach area had been captured on D-Day, and it was a major landing area for American troops. We moved in our trucks from the Beach to our assigned camping area.

We were lucky that we reached the camp without trouble. Our platoon commander first led the trucks beyond the camping area we were supposed to go to; in fact we drove beyond the front lines in that area. What made him realize we had gone too far was that when our group of trucks drove through a small French village on that road, we were cheered by the inhabitants. This was exciting and unexpected. The Lieutenant then checked his map of the Normandy front and realized we were beyond the front line. The villagers had cheered us because we were the first American troops they had seen, and it was Bastille Day. They thought we had liberated them from the Germans. They were wrong, but fortunately for us there were then no German troops in or near that village. We were able to drive back to where we should have stopped without any contact with the Germans. On our drive from the beach, we did see German planes overhead and several times we had to jump out of the trucks into ditches along the road because the planes were strafing the road, but we were not hit.

Soon after July 14th the Third Army broke out of Normandy to move across France, and our platoon was part of one of the armored divisions in that advance. I was not a skilled radio repairman myself, and I generally worked with another repairman who was a better worker than I was. The main technique I used was hitting both sides of a defective radio taken out of the tank in the hope that my blows would reconnect wires or parts that had been disconnected by bumps on the rough roads. Sometimes that worked, but not very often. Our armored division went across France that summer and fall., going as far east as Nancy where it camped until the next move.

Two non-military events occurred on that trip that I still remember. The first was a social event – a French farmer from one of the villages we passed through and in which we camped for several days invited all our platoon to have dinner at his home. It was a delicious home cooked meal, especially so after the portable army food we had been eating. While my French was poor, another of the soldiers could understand and speak it well, and we had a friendly conversation with our hosts. I was struck by the fact that this farmer had never left his village during his life, and I thought of the difference between his life and American lives in that respect. A second non-military event that I enjoyed was that we passed near recently liberated Paris on our way across France, and I and several others in our platoon were able to go there for a few hours. None of us had ever been there, but it was very pleasurable, not so much for the sights that we didn't know there, but rather because we were greeted so warmly when we spoke to anyone on the streets or in a store.

We had been in Nancy for only a short time when the Germans attacked the American and British Armies in the Battle of the Bulge. While Patton's Third Army was not the focus of the attack, the Army was moved north to help support the resistance to that attack. Not unexpectedly, in our move on the road we were strafed by German planes and had to leave our trucks for shelter in the ditches. The German attack was beaten back and after it the Allied Armies, including the Third, crossed the Rhine and on through Germany. In the Battle of the Bulge itself, several soldiers in the 187th Signal Company had been killed. In the battle against the German attack, soldiers were shifted from units not in the area of the attack to infantry units directly resisting the attack. In the 187th Company several of the men in the Headquarters Platoon were shifted to infantry units fighting the Germans directly. Several friends of mine had volunteered for that shift, and two of these were killed. In my opinion they were heroes. I wondered if I would have volunteered if I had been with the Headquarters platoon, rather than with an active armored division and away from the company headquarters.

After crossing the Rhine, we continued to move east to Frankfurt, Munich and eventually to the Czech border, moving back to Munich when the German war ended in mid-1945. We had no contact with German civilians during our military move east. We went through several cities; the bigger cities were hard hit by Allied bombing, but in several smaller towns old medieval churches were still intact. I remember that I saw very few German trucks and cars on the roads or in cities, in contrast to the large numbers of such vehicles in the American army, and thought that greater mobility probably helped us defeat the German armies. We did not pass through any of the concentration camps, and I did not see any of the freed Jewish and other prisoners from those camps, or bodies of murdered prisoners. But I did not want to meet any German civilians or troops of my generation and older, since I wondered what they had done during Hitler's rule and the war and what they knew and felt about the mass murder of the Jews, Gypsies, Poles and Russians during the war. Nor did I go back to Germany after the war until the late 1990's for the same reason. I did go then mainly to meet scholars in my field from the next generation and friends I had met in my work. I then did visit the Dachau Camp and several other Holocaust Memorials, and they were a shock.

In the U.S. itself during the time I served in Europe, the most moving event for me was the death of Franklin Roosevelt, which I heard of while in Germany. He was a great president whose goals and achievements in the United States and the world did so very much to shape America's post-war society and American aims for the world as a whole. He is for me the model of a great president, though in retrospect I disagree with what his administration did after Pearl Harbor to the Japanese-born American citizens and residents, forcing them into camps away from their homes, and the failure to do more to save the future Holocaust victims. But I knew little of the United States during my years and a half in Europe. Nor did I write much to my family about my experiences. I sent postcards to my parents and family in Brooklyn and Bridgeport, but said little personally except that I was well. I wanted them to know that, but didn't want to worry them about my war experience. There was not very much news to me from the family:

Helen and Sam had their son, and Paul had married my step-niece, Gladys, during my time away.

After the war ended in Europe, the different platoons of the 187th Signal Repair Company were reunited. We first returned from the Czech border to Munich for a few days and then for a longer stay in Frankfurt until our new orders would come. Both cities had been largely destroyed; we were mainly confined to our quarters and neighborhood. It was forbidden for us to have any social contact with the Germans beyond the necessary minimum. But some German civilians in our neighborhood did want to talk and some exchange with younger Germans was possible. I also knew some German language from my study in college and from my Yiddish so I could talk with them. I remember that some of those I did talk to predicted that we would be fighting with the Russians soon and my telling them I didn't think that would happen. While we were in Frankfurt, we learned that the Third Army would be going to the Pacific Theatre to be the army invading Japan, with whom we were still at war. The 187th Signal Repair Company, in the Third Army, would be in that invasion. Enroute to the Pacific Theatre we would go through the United States and have home leave before crossing the Pacific. In June we left Germany for England from where we sailed on the "Queen Elizabeth" to New York. This was a relatively quick and comfortable sea trip, and I did not get seasick. After our landing, we went to Fort Dix in New Jersey and then on our month home leaves.

I spent most of my home leave in Brooklyn with my mother and stepfather and with my stepsister and brothers living in Brooklyn. Ida and Sigmund, my stepsister and brother-in-law, and Gladys' parents took me with them for a few days to the Catskills at a pleasant resort. I also visited Bridgeport to see my Aunt and Uncle, Helen and Sam, and their children and Gertrude, who were then there. After home leave ended in late July, the company reassembled at Fort Jackson, South Carolina, to prepare for the move to the Pacific.

The war with Japan ended in August after the two atomic bombs were dropped on Hiroshima and Nagasaki and the Japanese surrendered. This was a complete and happy surprise to us – we had known nothing of the atomic bombs and all of us in the Company were very glad that their use had, by ending the war, saved us from what would have been a bloody invasion. (In retrospect I am glad the war ended when it did, and I am sure that ending saved many lives of American and Japanese troops and of Japanese civilians who would have been killed by conventional bombing. But I also wonder if dropping the second bomb on Nagasaki had been necessary for peace and if it might not have been avoided.)

We celebrated the ending of the war on the night we heard of that, by going to the local bar and getting drunk. Soon after, the Company moved to Fort Bragg in North Carolina where we received our discharges – mine was dated October 10, 1945. I could have re-enlisted in the Army Reserve, but I didn't want to do that. I didn't like the military atmosphere and discipline as a very small cog – an enlisted man – in a giant wheel in which I had little or no influence over what I did, and I did not like radio repair work. I separated entirely from the Army.

Looking back at my Army experience, I am glad that I had fought against Hitler and the Nazis and thus contributed personally to his downfall. I am also glad that I served with a mix of American soldiers from many social groups, though no blacks, I had not known before. I believe we worked well with each other, and I am sure this experience helped me to work with other people of different countries with whom I worked in later life. This experience overseas also contributed to my interest in, and willingness to, live and work in far different societies than the United States. I also learned that I have little interest or skill in mechanical work, confirming my intention to continue in Economics. With the extension of computers and electronics over the past 50 years, my lack of such skills, however, may be limiting my enjoyment of life today, but I don't see much pleasure from the new technologies on my part.

With my discharge in October 1945, I was able to return to the Princeton Graduate School in that Fall Term to refresh my Economics, which I had not used for 2 ½ years, to decide on a Ph.D. topic and start work on a thesis. My costs were covered by the GI Bill, and I lived in the Grad College.

During those years in the Army, there had been major changes in my family. My stepfather and mother had sold the store in Flatbush and purchased a smaller store in Downtown Brooklyn on Fulton Street. They also moved from their old apartment to one very near the new store. This new store was run by them alone; my step-brother Morris did not work there and had other work.

My Bridgeport family also went through major changes. Helen and Sam moved to north Bridgeport, building a new house there, and my uncle and aunt, Helen's parents, also decided to move and build another house next to Helen and Sam's. Helen was teaching and Sam practicing law. They had two children, Judy and Andy, and soon after the war they had a third child, Richard. Walter had worked in the U.S. government in Washington during the war. He had married Charlotte Hoffman, a Vassar graduate, and they had their first child, Robert. Paul left the Air Force after the war, and he entered Rensselaer Polytechnic Institute in Troy, New York, to refresh his engineering, and he and Gladys had moved there. Gertrude, the youngest of my cousins, two years younger than I, finished college and started graduate school. Clearly the year right after the war was a year of change for all of us as we began new and peaceful lives.

CHAPTER III

Starting My Career

A. Refreshing my Economics and Writing my Thesis

I HAD DONE no Economics for three years in the Army and had forgotten some of what I had learned before. Returning to Princeton, I again took courses in Economic Theory with Professors Friedrich Lutz and Morgenstern. Professor Morgenstern had just published the book *The Theory of Games and Economic Behavior* with Professor Von Neumann, and I studied that book in that year and found it very interesting, but I did not use it in my later work. Apart from the courses I took, I explored various ideas for my Ph.D. Thesis. With my earlier interest in Labor Economics, I discussed possible labor topics with Professors Brown, McCabe and Lester. Another area of interest was a topic in a field that was, or would be, important in a broader public policy area. I discussed a possible topic with Professor Graham, and he suggested one that interested me very much after my wartime international experience.

He anticipated that after the war many of the colonies would become independent and would aim to develop economically. If India became independent and sought to develop economically, and if China, which was independent, also sought a similar economic goal, what would be the effect of the development of two such large countries upon the United States? The Japanese experience and development after its opening to the world and international trade in the Nineteenth Century might serve as a guide to the future India-China development effects on trade and the American economy. If I accepted that suggestion, I would be able to combine my specific interests in international trade and economic history within a broader framework of institutional economics and a public-policy approach, all of which appealed to me. I decided to choose that topic, under the guidance of Professor Graham, whom I considered both a very able and intellectually stimulating economist and teacher.

I began my research at Princeton. I would be relying entirely on material available in the United States without any experience or research on my part in India, China or Japan; all three of which were going through periods of major political change after the war. Fortunately two Princeton faculty members, William Lockwood in History and Marion Levy in Sociology, were respectively major scholars on Japan and China. They had each just published important books on those countries, and their research and personal availability were very helpful for my work. At the same time, the Princeton Office of Population Research, headed by Professor Frank Notestein, with Ansley Coale, Kingsley Davis and Dudley Kirk on its staff, was doing path-breaking research on population trends in China and India and their world economic impact. This provided useful data and insights for my own research on future economic trends for both countries.

In writing my thesis, I planned to project India's and China's changing comparative advantage in international trade as they industrialized over time. They would also be growing in population, and both of these trends would increase their demands for food for their people and raw material inputs for their industrial outputs and for economic capital and skilled labor, and possibly contribute to expanding exports of their outputs. My thesis would seek to explore and analyze the effects of such changes upon the American economy. The chapters on the future of Indian and Chinese development would be preceded by a review of the Japanese economic development since the 1850's and the economic effect of that development upon the American economy, relying upon the earlier work of economists and social scientists for history and data.

I finished my thesis in 1949, writing most of it while I was teaching at Bard College after physically leaving Princeton in 1946. Fortunately Bard was close enough to New York and Princeton that I could use the research facilities and material in both those cities. Also if I had problems, I could, and would, contact Professor Graham for his advice, and I would send him penciled drafts of chapters for criticism and suggestions. I had good handwriting – he could read those drafts, and he was willing to so do. I did not type, and Professor Graham understood the expense I would incur in order to get those drafts typed. (I cannot imagine that any of today's faculty would be willing to read penciled drafts of a thesis – I would not.)

The thesis was completed in Spring 1949, submitted in the typed form required, reviewed and accepted by the Economics Department, and I received my Princeton Ph.D. in June. It was fortunate that I did finish then because Frank Graham died in the fall of that same year, and I had been his last Ph.D. student. Working under his guidance was the major intellectual experience of my life until then, and the thesis itself was the foundation of my career. As I wrote in the preface to the thesis, "his constant searching criticism, his insistent demand for skepticism, clarity and sharpness, his willingness to devote his time to reading the numerous drafts and criticizing them . . . , and his general kindliness throughout the entire period have been of inestimable aid to me . . . [and] it made the writing of the thesis the most valuable intellectual experience that [I had until then] undergone." His treatment of me as his student was a model for me in my relationship to my students when I taught graduate students later.

Apart from this thesis writing experience, Frank Graham's ideas with respect to the character of Economics and the role of the economist in society, which he had first presented in his classes before I entered the Army, were strongly emphasized when I worked closely with him on my thesis. That role was to influence public policy to make a better-working economy and society, thereby raising the well-being of all the people. For Economics to perform this Public Policy function the economist must also understand the wider society of which the economy is one part, and that society should be understood by a broader value system than simply the aim of maximizing personal and enterprise gain. It is also necessary to understand the political system within which policy is made if policy is to be influenced. Economics is thus Political Economy in what had been the British historical sense from Adam Smith through Keynes. For this function it must also be written in a language the general public and policy makers understand. It was not for him, nor for me, the Mathematical Model Building exercise that it has become since the Second World War. John Kenneth Galbraith, who knew Frank Graham at Princeton when he taught there, wrote very warmly of Graham's contribution to Economics in a recent volume.

Apart from the effect of my work with Frank Graham upon my philosophy with respect to economics, my following Frank Graham's topic suggestion had a direct effect upon my future career and life. Before I wrote that thesis, I would never have predicted I would work for the rest of my life on Asian economies and therefore live in various Asian countries for many years.

B. Teaching at Bard

I began teaching at Bard in the Fall of 1946 after a summer of teaching Introductory Economics at the College of William and Mary. That college is in Williamsburg, Virginia, and being at that old historical capitol of the state was an enjoyable experience. That was my first college teaching work. I was substituting for a permanent faculty member in the summer, and that was useful for my next, longer-term teaching job. That job would be at Bard.

Bard College was a unique college unlike any other academic institution I have since known, in a very positive sense. At the time, 1946-1950, it had about 250 students and about 30 faculty members in its different departments. In Economics there was one other faculty member, Adolf Sturmthal, who was the senior and tenured faculty.

Adolf had been born and educated in Vienna where he had studied with Eugen von Böhm-Bawerk at the University of Vienna. Böhm-Bawerk was one of the leading economists of the Austrian school, and his students included, among others, Professors Haberler and Machlup who had been contemporaries of Adolf's. Unlike them Adolf did not go into academic life after graduating; he joined the Austrian Socialist Party in which he held a major post, and then in the 1930's, after Austria became a dictatorship, he moved to Switzerland to become a leading official in the Second Socialist International. He left Switzerland in the late 1930's for the United States. Before 1941 he had entered academic life in New York, first at Columbia University and then at Bard, which was part of Columbia before the War. When the U.S. entered the war, he worked on Germany and the West European War in the Office of War Information in Washington. He returned to Bard as Economics Professor when the war ended. His field of specialization was Labor Economics, based on his interest and earlier experience in Europe. His interests and experience fitted in well with my interests, and this for me was a great plus, although I did not expect that when I decided to teach at Bard.

Bard was a progressive college – classes were small, there were close relations between students and faculty. Each student had an individual faculty advisor in his or her field whom he or she met for an individual tutorial in that field. (This was modeled on the Oxford tutorial system.) There was also close social exchange among all the faculty across disciplines since we almost all lived on campus or in the small local community.

In my first years there I lived in an off-campus house with another young faculty member, Robie Macauley, who was in the English Department. We became good friends, and knowing Robie broadened my knowledge and experience widely in many fields other than Economics. Robie had a great knowledge of English and other European literature, both classical and contemporary, and he introduced me to many of the great novelists and poets by his recommendations. He had been a student at Kenyon before the war when that college was one of the leading American centers of literary studies and creative writing. He was a fellow student of Robert Lowell and Randall Jarrell, among others. I met them and other friends when they visited him at Bard, and

I also read their works. Robie was also a lover of opera, and listening to his records of Mozart and Verdi contributed to my love of opera. I first went to the opera to see Verdi's "The Masked Ball," one of my favorites, playing in New York. Robie and I remained in close touch until Robie died several years ago. Other members of the English Department whom I got to know there and whose later works I have read were Fred Dupee, Ted Weiss, Harvey Shapiro, Bill Humphrey and James Merrill, all of whom taught at Bard during my five years there. Bard also had good art and theatre departments. I met Stefan Hirsch, a contemporary German artist who had left after the Nazis came to power. Stefan by conversation and his own work introduced me to German Expressionism and the Bauhaus artists. Richard Burns and Claire Leonard were teaching theatre and music, and Bard also had a strong ballet program. Joseph Precker was a starting faculty member in Psychology, and we have remained in contact since, though far distant from each other in many parts of the world. Another young faculty member during the later part of my time there was Paul DeMan. We became friends and we socialized freely with each other, other faculty and students. We did not stay in touch after I left Bard, and later he went to Yale. He made a significant contribution to contemporary philosophy while at Yale, but after his death he was accused of having been anti-Semitic and pro-Nazi while living in Belgium during the Nazi occupation before he left for Latin America. One of his older relatives had been an important Belgian supporter of the Nazis at that time. In my contact with him, and from what I saw of his relations with other faculty and students, I saw and heard no anti-Semitism or pro-Fascism in his expressed opinions or actions.

During my time at Bard, the female students were especially good students. I think parents did not object to sending their daughters to a progressive college like Bard, strong in the arts, while they preferred sending their sons to the Ivy League colleges, which might also still be restricted to males. I remember I did have some good students in Economics, but I also met socially some very good women students in the Arts Departments. I was a close friend of one, Rhoda Levine, studying Theatre and Dance at the time, and we have been in touch in recent years. She has been teaching and directing theatre and opera at Northwestern University, near Chicago, for some years.

In retrospect the interaction among faculty across many disciplines that was possible at Bard, as well as with students, is unusual in the larger academic institutions I've been connected with since then. In the larger institutions I met faculty in other fields largely by chance or by serving on committees with them. I think the decline of such exchange, since I studied at Princeton and taught at Bard in the 1940's, is a loss by reducing the breadth of ideas and approaches to their work among faculty, thus reducing the benefits of academic work and teaching.

I was also glad to teach Economics at Bard because Adolf Sturmthal was a very stimulating and supportive colleague. His own approach to Economics, with a policy oriented focus, was similar to mine. His socialist background and work in Labor Economics was evidence of the relevance of that approach. His early book *The Tragedy of European Labor 1918-1939* is a pioneer study of the policy experience of European socialism after the First World War, and how the failures of the socialist parties in dealing with the 1930's Depression contributed to the rise and spread of Fascism in Germany and wider Europe. Adolf and I became good friends on both a personal and professional level, and I got to know his family, living on the campus also. Our friendship continued after I left Bard, and later when Adolf had moved to the University of Illinois at Urbana Economics Department.

Another advantage of Bard at the time was that in two or three months of winter the students were on intern programs off campus so that there was no teaching. This made it possible for me to spend five to six consecutive months of each year (broken into winter and summer) on my own work writing my thesis and completing it in three years.

Bard's closeness to New York City and the ease of train transportation between Rhinebeck and New York made it possible too to visit with my parents in Brooklyn and good friends in Manhattan. I also went often to plays, concerts and museums in New York City. At the time my closest woman friend, Garland Draper, was Robie's sister-in-law. She worked in New York and lived in Greenwich Village. She was beautiful, and we had many interests in common in literature, theatre and music.

She did not want to marry, and over time, as I left Bard, moved to Washington and then worked overseas, our relationship weakened and we eventually separated.

Bard then had only one tenured Economics faculty member, Adolf, and one not tenured. I left after five years, in 1951. I was psychologically ready for that move, since I wanted to get some non-academic policy-influencing experience. I applied for a Civil Service (not Foreign Service) post in the U.S. State Department, which was looking for an economist to work in the Japan section of the Office of Intelligence Research (OIR). With my research on the Japanese economy for my thesis I was hired, though I had never been there until then.

I was now over 30 years old. Joseph Schumpeter had once said that by the age of 30 a thinker should have written a major work. I had not, and I wanted experience that would yield such a work.

CHAPTER IV

Japan – My First International Economic Work

I N 1951 THE State Department, with Dean Acheson as Secretary of State, was playing a major policy role both in reconstructing the war-torn European and Asian economies, and in creating a new world order resisting Communist advances on both continents. Within the department the Office of Intelligence and Research did not engage in the immediate problems before the country desks, but rather carried out longer range analysis and research on country and regional issues, although assisting on short-term issues if necessary. The Japan Division of OIR was dealing with the political issue of the transition from U.S. Occupation to democratic self-government, and with the appropriate economic policies for an independent economy.

The head of the OIR Japan office was a political specialist, Bill Jones, who had been in the Pacific Theater during the War, and worked in Japan after it. The economics section, in which I worked, was headed by Leonard Felsenthal, a very able economist who had migrated from Nazi Germany in the 1930's, studied Economics at the University of Chicago, and served in Europe and the Occupation of Germany during and after the war. He then joined the Foreign Service, working as an economist, assigned to problems of the Japanese economy during the Occupation.

The OIR Asian Division at that time had some of the leading American social scientists working on Asian political and economic issues. Among those I first met then were Cora Dubois, who later left to join Radcliffe's Anthropology Department, where she later supervised the Harvard Ph.D. thesis of Sylvia Vatuk, my future wife. Another Economic colleague in OIR's China Division was Alex Eckstein, who later left for Harvard and then Michigan, where he first headed the China program there. We remained close friends, exchanging ideas, as long as he lived. Other able economists and political scientists then in OIR and in the Foreign Service, who remained in the State Department and became Ambassadors to, and senior State Department policy-making officials dealing with, Asian countries. These included Ed Fried, Jack Lydman, Phil Trezise, Brad Coolidge, Tom Shoesmith and Martin Hirabayashi. My experience in working with these highly intelligent and experienced officials gave me an insight into policy-making techniques and problems that both tied in very closely to my own interest in a policy-oriented economic approach, and was very valuable for my future economic work. It also reinforced my strong belief in writing my work in a language and style that could be read by a reader who was not a mathematician or an economist, but interested in, or making, public policy.

In the early 1950's the main economic issue that the OIR Japan section was working on was the post-occupation future of the Japanese economy. Would the economic reforms and policies introduced under American rule be sufficient to prevent a collapse of the economy without American support and also stimulate the longer term growth of the economy? Looking back fifty years later when Japan had become one of the world's leading economic powers, that question seems ironic, but that fifty years economic experience may be a sign of Japan's own pre-war economic history and post-war policy judgment, as well as the success of the occupation policies. In the immediate short-run, American military spending in Japan for the Korean War helped the Japanese economy support itself after the Occupation and to gain the resources for its later growth.

As part of my job in OIR I was sent to Japan in early 1952, before the actual end of the Occupation, to write a report on the future of Japan's industrial sector. My stay there overlapped the end of the Occupation and the restart of self-government. In my work there I met many of Japan's leading economists, in and out of the government, private industrialists, bankers and industrial policy-making government officials. I also visited many factories in a wide group of industries ranging from textiles to manufacture of machinery and final products of various types. I was struck by the close interaction among the industrialists, bankers and officials, closer than in the U.S., and the positive effect this was having on Japan's industrial recovery and expansion. Among the industrialists there was a strong interest in technological changes in other countries in the production of their products. I was told that in the past Japanese industrialists had been able to effectively combine local and foreign technologies from many countries to achieve a unique and profitable Japanese production process and final product that had contributed to Japan's pre-war industrial success. I met, among the Japanese economists, Shigeto Tsuru, a former classmate of Kenneth Galbraith and Paul Sweezy at Harvard, and Saburo Okita and Takeshi Watanabe. All three were then in important policy-making positions, and the latter two played key roles in founding and running the Asian Development Bank in the later 1960's.

The Americans working in Japan at the time were a distinguished group, and I knew some of them well. Wolf Ladejinsky was the economist who played a major role in formulating the land reform policy introduced during the Occupation which contributed significantly to the success of Japan's economy after the war and which also served as a model for land reform in South Korea and Taiwan; Wolf also advised the Indian government on land reform policy. William Gilmartin and Orville McDiarmid also worked on the Economic staff of the Occupation, later joining the World Bank as top economic officers, working particularly on and in India. I remained good friends with the three of them for the rest of their lives.

Among the non-economist U.S. Embassy Foreign Service officers, I got to know Richard Finn, a senior political scientist, who later wrote one of the best books I know on American policy in Japan during the Occupation, and Edward Seidensticker. He later left the Foreign Service for the University of Michigan, where he was one of the leading American scholars of classical Japanese literature, and translated the classic *Tales of Genji*.

My work in Japan itself contributed greatly not only to my direct knowledge of Japanese industry, but to an understanding of the Japanese industrialization process and the importance of technological change in that growth and of the institutional structure within which industry functioned. These insights and my visits to Japanese factories and meetings with industrialists were very useful for my research on industry in India and other Asian countries after 1955.

Apart from my economic work on this visit I had my first experience of Japanese culture. I stayed at the Frank Lloyd Wright designed Imperial Hotel in Tokyo which was very convenient for walking about the garden areas, shopping centers and Imperial Palace sections of the city. I visited Nara and Kyoto, which had not been bombed and had beautiful traditional temples and palace buildings and which then retained their traditional characters, and I also visited Mount Fuji to see its beauty. I also went to Hiroshima to see that city after the atomic bombing. The destruction there was very great, and that visit reinforced my hope that atomic bombs will never be used again. On these trips I stayed at traditional Japanese hotels and moved about easily – people were most helpful to someone like myself, largely ignorant of the language.

Apart from these travels I went to Japanese theatre in Tokyo to see Noh and Kabuki plays, which I enjoyed. I also went to Japanese art museums and galleries. I like Japanese art work and purchased some prints both older and by contemporary artists such as Munakata. Wolf Ladejinsky had a great knowledge of, and pleasure in, Japanese art and was a great guide to that art. I also developed a taste for Japanese food, especially sushi, and learned, in the restaurants, to eat with chopsticks. I still remember the great amusement the Japanese waitresses showed as they watched me struggle with chopsticks, and so they helped me eat with them.

On my return flight to the United States from Japan I decided to fly west stopping at other Asian and European cities I had not seen before. I took leave for the trip and stopped first at Hong Kong, then a British colony and a small and beautiful city. I could not then go to

Mainland China which had recently become a Communist country. From Hong Kong I went to Bangkok, then described as the "Venice of the Orient" with its numerous canals. I visited various Buddhist temples and royal palaces in and near the city which were very attractive. The change in the city from that time to today has been very great; today it is a tourist and business center in which sight-seeing is difficult and walking can be dangerous.

From Bangkok I flew to India, for my first visit, to Calcutta and Delhi. Calcutta was the poorest city I saw on the trip. I knew no one in the city and the hotel I stayed at, "The Great Eastern," was besieged by beggars who surrounded you at the hotel entrance begging for money. The sense of poverty was overwhelming. (This impression of Calcutta was far different than my view of Calcutta a decade later, when I lived there for a year.) I went to Delhi from Calcutta and in Delhi I had a pleasant stay at the Imperial Hotel. I was able to visit various Mogul Emperors' tombs and palaces in the city itself. I also went to see the Taj Mahal in Agra which was as beautiful as its reputation, and the old city of Fatehpur Sikhri, the Muslim capital built when Akbar was ruler and a striking monument to his rule.

From Delhi I flew to Istanbul, a very attractive city with its beautiful palaces and the great art of its museums. After India, I felt a marked sense of a better quality of material life and that impression remained throughout the rest of Europe. From there I flew to Athens to see the classic Greek buildings and art. The Parthenon was the most beautiful building I had seen, and I could now understand the glory of ancient Greece and its greatness in world history. I then went to Rome, whose historical monuments, palaces and great works of art were overwhelming. I was struck too by the apparent ease the people of Rome seemed to show living in the midst of their great city of art and history. I went from Rome to Paris to once again visit Notre Dame, Arc de Triomphe and the Louvre and then to London. When I had been in England in the war, I had not been able to spend any time there since it was not in the permitted travel radius of Banbury, where I had been camped. Now I could see and enjoy the city. I was staying at a good hotel near its center and was able to get about easily by public transportation and walking. Being able to speak English with people I met was a great advantage and pleasure. London with its great museums, historical buildings and areas and parks was a most enjoyable city, and I looked forward to future visits. The entire trip with its visits in Asia and Europe was a great experience introducing me to various cultures, ways of life and histories different from those of the United States. I would want more of such experiences if the opportunity arose.

After the travel and being away from family and friends for about six months, it was good to resettle in my Washington apartment and to again see my family in Brooklyn and Bridgeport. But Washington was on the verge of major political change with the forthcoming 1952 election. The Republicans won that election, Dwight Eisenhower replaced Harry Truman as President in March 1953 and John Foster Dulles replaced Dean Acheson as Secretary of State. Attacks on State Department officers by Republican Senator McCarthy for their supposed pro-Communism and for the "loss of China" had been very strong before the 1952 election, but Dean Acheson had resisted them. McCarthy's influence on the actual staffing in the Department was important under the new Republican administration.

The State Department's budget was cut, and there was an intensive search for supposed Communist sympathizers. As a result, there was a significant "reduction in force (riffing)" in the department. During this time, John Service and John Paton Davies, who had served in China and had been accused by Senator McCarthy of pro-Communism, were forced out, and others were cut for security or budget reasons. The cut-backs for budget reasons were largely concentrated among non-foreign service officers. OIR was affected by these cuts, and I was among those "riffed." I might have been able to stay on because of greater seniority than some of my colleagues. However, I was willing to be cut since they were married or had other dependents, and the blow of being cut would have been harder for them than for me, since I was young and single.

I was out of the State Department by late 1953 and had begun looking for another job before then. I applied to the U.N. for work in a new agency working in Korea and to various private firms with international interests. I had no luck with either of those directions.

With respect to the U.N., I learned later that my application had been held up by order of J. Edgar Hoover. (In 1995 I had requested and received my FBI files and learned this.) He ordered a full-scale security check on me in connection with that application. This may have been triggered by my going to Brooklyn College in the 1930's as well as my State Department employment under Dean Acheson. That FBI security check included interviews with my teachers at Brooklyn College and Princeton, with former colleagues in all the organizations and places, including Tokyo, where I had worked and with friends in those places. This took a long time and may have been a reason for my not hearing from the U.N. From the records I saw in 1995, all the people interviewed in 1954 with respect to my "communism" when they knew me, said I had not been earlier, and was not then, a communist supporter. I never had any other problem with security clearance.

In mid-1954 I received an offer from a private research organization, the Council for Economic and Industrial Research, that was preparing an Input-Output Table for the U.S.S.R. For this I got the required security clearance. One of the advisors on this project was Professor Wassily Leontief, then at Harvard, the founder of Input-Output analysis. Two of my fellow staff members with the Council were Joseph Berliner and Elizabeth Bass, both of whom became close friends. Both were economists who had worked on the Soviet economy previously and who knew Russian and who later made significant contributions to the study of Russia's economy. Since I was neither a Russian expert nor a statistician while working at the Council, I was also looking for another job with work more in line with my earlier training and experience.

In early 1955 I learned of the MIT Center for International Studies project on the economic development of India, Indonesia and Southern Italy and appropriate U.S. policy to aid those development efforts. I applied for the industrial economist position on the India project, and on the basis of my thesis and my work in Japan for the State Department, I was chosen. In June 1955 I left Washington for Cambridge and the MIT Center to learn about the project I was on.

While my Washington experience had been a mixed one, it had been a very valuable one. My Japan experience, both in the State Department and in Japan itself, was my first economic work both overseas and operational in the sense of influencing decision-making. I enjoyed it and also found I worked well in a foreign environment. One of the major benefits was that I had to write reports and papers for policy purposes and for non-economists. That meant they had to be to the point and in good English, understandable to readers who were not economists. I had to transcend the purely academic language in my professional writing, and I am glad I have that ability. I had also, on the basis of my actual research in Japan, written my first academic journal article, "Japanese Industry Since the War" published in the *Quarterly Journal of Economics* in 1953. This was followed by an article, based on my Ph.D. thesis, on Indian and Chinese industrialization, published in *Economic Development and Cultural Change* in 1954.[1]

Apart from supporting my policy-oriented economic approach, this Washington and Japan experience strongly reinforced my institutional approach to Economics. To influence policy-making I had to understand a broader horizon than the narrow economic one. Policy in any country is made within a social, historical and political framework. An economist, within a national or international agency, advising a government or an academic carrying on economic policy research in a country, must understand that wider framework within the country he or she is working. There is no single economic truth or path valid for any country any time. This experience strongly reinforced what I had learned from Theresa Wolfson and Frank Graham.

There were of course other major benefits of my three years in Washington. I made long-term friends with Leonard Felsenthal and his future wife, Floralee, and with Alex and Ruth Eckstein, and these friendships have been great pleasures in my life as long as my friends were alive. It was in Washington, too, that I learned to drive, got a driver's license and bought my first car, and that has benefited me since. Finally, Washington was a center of music and theatre. The Budapest String Quartet was playing at the Library of Congress. That quartet was one of the world's greatest and hearing them shaped my prime enjoyment of music ever since.

---

[1] Both these articles are reprinted in my book *Economic Development in Asia* (Avebury, 1996), pp. 25 - 44 for the Japan article and pp. 6 - 24 for the India/China article.

CHAPTER V

Almost a Decade in India and Nepal

A. With The MIT Center Project, 1955 1960

THE MIT CENTER for International Studies (CENIS) was founded by Max Millikan in 1950 to do research on international issues important for the United States then and in the future. Max Millikan had come to MIT after some years of service in U.S. government policy-making research; another member of the MIT Economic faculty then was Walt Rostow, a leading economic historian, who had also had an important policy-research role in Europe during the Second World War, and was very interested in the economic development of the newly independent countries and the implications of their development for the United States. They initiated a major research project examining the economic development of India, Indonesia and Southern Italy to explore the problems and requirements for their economic development, and appropriate American policy to support their efforts.

Paul Rosenstein-Rodan, a founder of the field of economic development, became the head of the Southern Italy project; Wilfred Malenbaum, a distinguished agricultural economist, the head of the India project; and Ben Higgins, a major international economist, the head of the Indonesian project. All had extensive policy-related work during and after the war.

India, with its great size and its democratic newly independent government, was seen as a counter-model of development to the newly established Chinese communist government. India's success would guide other newly independent countries to democratic rather than dictatorial policy paths of economic development. Hopefully, the Indonesian experience would contribute toward the same goal, while South Italian experience under the re-established Italian democracy would indicate that a Fascist dictatorial path was unnecessary for economic development.

The purpose of my summer at MIT before leaving for India was both to learn and explore the broader field of economic development, and more specifically India's economic history and policy goals and achievements since independence, to plan my own research on its industrial policy problems and directions. My Ph.D. had not been based on any experience in India itself, or any research there.

At the MIT Center at the time was Andrew Brimmer who had just returned from a year in India working on his Harvard Ph.D. on issues of industrial growth there. Helen Lamb was an important staff member on the India project. She was herself both knowledgeable on Indian economic history and policy issues, and knew well some of the major American and Indian social scientists and historians working on India at Harvard and elsewhere in this country. She introduced me to P.N. Dhar, then in residence at Harvard, and his wife, Sheila, whose friendship was of great value for my economic work in India and my appreciation of Indian culture. Helen also introduced me to John Kenneth Galbraith at Harvard, with whose broader approach to Economics I very much agreed, and who was very much interested in India's development. Through Helen I met Daniel and Alice Thorner in Bombay soon after arriving there. Another very valuable friend from Bombay whom I met, then studying at MIT, was George Coelho, a graduate of Bombay University. George introduced me to his parents living in Bombay and his former teacher, Professor Kamal Wood and her husband, Evelyn Wood, a former English official and businessman in colonial and independent India. They all introduced me to far broader aspects of India's society and culture than narrowly economic ones.

I also met that summer at MIT several students writing Ph.D. theses on aspects of India's economy who were going to India for their research. These included Subbiah Kannappan and Phil Kotler, and we remained in contact in India, exchanging ideas there and after. I have remained friends with them ever since. Dick Eckaus and Francis Bator were at the Center and MIT, and we exchanged ideas on my forthcoming research. Thus that Cambridge summer was a good preparation for the upcoming year in India itself.

I got to New Delhi in early September. Bill Malenbaum was already there, and he introduced me to economists of the Planning Commission and at Delhi University. I met Tarlok Singh, the Secretary and central administrator on the Planning Commission, who expressed interest in reading my work for its possible use by the Commission, as the research moved along. At the University I met some of India's leading economists, Professors V.K.R.V. Rao, K.N. Raj, and B.N. Ganguly among others, all playing a significant role in India's planning, who were both interested in my work and had useful suggestions. As a result of my thinking and conversations in Cambridge that summer, and the very useful exchange of ideas with the economists in Delhi, my research ideas had broadened. Originally it had been a fairly narrow project focusing on the investment requirements, estimated by calculating capital/output ratios for key industries, to achieve India's future industrial output goals, both in the private and public sectors. Now I saw the project as an overview of the broader climate and policy issues related to India's industrial growth, of which capital requirements, and measures to raise them, were only one aspect.

Bill Malenbaum, on visits to Bombay before I went there, had established a connection for me with the Bombay University Economics Department, one of India's best, and with the Director of the Association of Trade and Industry, Dr. K.R. Paymaster, in the city. That Association had good contacts with many of the country's major industrialists operating in and near Bombay. I was given office space at the Association, located near the University, and I was in regular contact with Economic Department faculty and scholars, as well as Association staff. I was invited by both the Economics Department and the Association to participate in faculty and other appropriate functions. Both of these institutions, as well as the small apartment I rented, were in, or very near to, Downtown Bombay. The Reserve Bank of India (RBI), the Bombay Stock Exchange, and offices of major private industrial firms such as the Tata's, major banks, and important government offices were located in that area and all were easy to reach. The textile factories of Bombay's then leading industry, and other factories also, were in other parts of town as was the seaport area, but I could get to them easily to visit them and interview owners, managers, and even some trade union officials. (I only knew English and that set limits on interviewing.)

I received strong support for my research from the Bombay University Economics Department faculty. Professors Vakil, Lakdawala, Dantwala and Brahmananda were all working on issues of India's economic development and were very helpful by their insights into issues, research suggestions, and comments. I also gave several seminars in the Economics Department on my work as it moved along and benefited by the interchange. I may have been helpful too in putting some of the younger faculty in touch with economists in the Planning Commission whom they may not have met as yet.

The economists at the Reserve Bank of India (RBI) were also very supportive of my research. I was in regular contact with Dr. B.K. Madan, who headed the RBI's Economic Research division. I had also been introduced by Alvin Karchere, my pre-war Brooklyn College and Princeton classmate, to Dr. K.S. Krishnaswamy, one of the Bank's senior economists, who was a post-war classmate of Al's at the London School of Economics (LSE). Krishnaswamy, too, had been on the Planning Commission staff when it was first set up, before he moved to RBI, so he was very aware of the major Indian planning issues. We became very good friends, and he not only was an excellent critic of my work, but he introduced me to other economists at the RBI and in Bombay, as well as to other sides of Indian culture than the economic. Through him I met V.V. Bhatt, D.R. Khatkhate and M. Narasimhan at the Bank, all of whom were most helpful for both my current research and my

1958-1959 work in Bombay. Dr. Paymaster and Phiroze Medhora at the Association of Trade and Industry were also most helpful both for their suggestion for, and comments on, my work. They also put me in touch with private industrialists and businessmen in the Bombay area, whom I could interview and whose factories I was able to visit.

Bill Malenbaum had earlier hired a young Indian economist, Dr. A. Vaidyanathan, who had received his Economics Ph.D. from Cornell University, to work with me. Vaidyanathan had decided that he would return to India to work on India's development problems after he got his Ph.D., and we worked together during that year. His work was very valuable for my research and for my broader knowledge of India not only that first year, but for all my later work on the Indian economy, He became one of India's leading economists, especially in the agricultural development area, and he directed major research programs in South India in Kerala and in Madras, from where he came and where he worked later in his career.

Several other young economists then working on their Ph.D's at Bombay University, R.K. Hazari and J.C. Sandesara, later Professors there, became good friends and were valuable sources of insight and criticism as my work progressed. I have been friends with them and their families since. Apart from academic and government economists, the person who gave me the most useful sense of broader Indian society as well as the greatest assistance in my work was Sachin Chaudhuri, the founder and Editor of the "Economic Weekly," one of India's leading journals on its economic development and political and social issues and policies. (The comparable western journal in its broad appeal is "The Economist," but with a different political viewpoint.) Sachin was from Bengal and Calcutta and was a striking example of the Calcutta intellectual aliveness and leadership. He was a central figure in bringing Indian thought to bear on the broad issues of India's political and economic development, and its hopes, and policies. (After his death, the journal became "The Economic and Political Weekly," the EPW, edited by Krishna Raj, who maintained its leading role for ideas on Indian policy.) Sachin welcomed fresh ideas and research for publication by both Indian and foreign scholars and policy influencers. I published several articles in "Economic Weekly" in my two years in Bombay, and we were very good friends both in India and on his American visits. Sachin's Bombay apartment was a center for great Bengali meals and for meeting his numerous friends from India and all over the world. Two of his close friends, originally from Calcutta, were A.K. Das Gupta, then one of the country's leading academic economists, and Ashok Mitra, then a leading government economist and later Finance Minister in the Communist Party government of West Bengal.

The introduction that George Coelho gave me to the Woods was extremely valuable, not only in terms of meeting a family that I enjoyed very much, but in introducing me to an active Bombay culture and to other people who became close long time friends. Kamal Wood's sister, Shirin, is the wife of one of India's leading contemporary painters, Jehangir Sabavala. I like his paintings very much, and, by his work and that of other artists in the galleries he is associated with, I became acquainted with contemporary Indian painters. The Indian art scene is a very active one, and I am very glad that Indian and other South Asian art has now reached the broader world-wide audience that it has long deserved. Jehangir's brother Sharokh was the India correspondent of "The Christian Science Monitor" in the 1950's and later a top official of the Tata's industrial establishment. His help was very useful for my research on industrial policy. It was through the Sabavalas that I had a sense of great Parsi contributions not only to India's economic life, but to its cultural life as well.

The Woods were also close friends of Maurice and Taya Zinkin, then living in Bombay. Maurice had been a senior ICS officer in the British government of India during the war and in the transition to India's independence, and had then joined Unilever's Hindustan Lever Company in Bombay as one of its top officers. Taya was the "Manchester Guardian" correspondent in India, and both were well acquainted with major political and business leaders in the country and with India's political and economic scene. Maurice was one of the most stimulating and provocative thinkers I knew on India's history and contemporary problems and talking with him was always very useful as well as enjoyable. The Zinkins were good friends of A.D. Gorwala and H.M. Patel, also former ICS officers, before and after independence, whose knowledge of the working of India's political system and economy was unique. I became a good friend of Gorwala, whom I called "Uncle." Visiting him in Bombay was always a pleasure and stimulating. He founded "Opinion" magazine in his later years, a small journal which was one of the most courageous magazines I knew for its ideas on the current scene. Through Maurice and Taya I met Prakash and Ingrid Tandon, also living in Bombay. Prakash was a top Hindustan Lever officer, becoming its first Indian head. His knowledge of India – its society, politics and economy – was very great, and his insights into various aspects of events in all those areas were most useful. His autobiography with its picture of the partition of colonial India into Independent India and Pakistan, and of his family's move to the new India after 1947, gives a unique insight into that partition and its personal effects, as well as later events in his lifetime. I have just heard, while writing this, the sad news of his death at 93. Finally, it was at the Zinkin's that I first met Scarlett Epstein, the first anthropologist I met working in India in a village in South India, and my friend since. Scarlett's work on the village, changing conditions there and relationships between that village and nearby cities provided new insights into India's rural economic and social system and growth process. I visited that village later that year during Scarlett's work there; it was my first visit to rural India, which was and is the main sector of Indian society in terms of numbers of people living and working there.

So far I have not mentioned the Americans I was working with in India on the Center project, nor other Americans I met in Bombay or Delhi. The American economist working for the MIT project on India's agriculture sector was Walter Neale ("Terry" Neale to his friends). Terry was based at the Gokhale Institute in Pune, about 100 miles from Bombay. The Gokhale Institute, headed by Professor D.R. Gadgil, was one of India's leading economic research institutes on rural problems with a very able professional staff. Terry was an institutional economist with a training in Indian economic history at the London School of Economics with Vera Anstey, one of England's leading scholars on India. He had also done work on Indian social issues before he joined the project, and was very knowledgeable of those issues in the rural sector. He and I strongly agreed on a broad institutional approach to economic issues. We became good friends and had a close exchange of ideas on our research in India, and remained close personal friends beyond our professional connection, until he died very recently.

Helen Lamb had given me Dan Thorner's address in Bombay, and Bill Malenbaum urged me to look him up. I did so soon after I got there – he and his wife, Alice, were good friends of Sachin and all the Indian economists I knew, and Terry knew Dan's work well. Dan had done pioneer work on India's economic history before the war and had worked on India for the U.S. government during the war. He had then been in the University of Pennsylvania's History Department on the South Asia program there. In the 1950's he was doing research in India, when he was accused of communism during the McCarthy period. The University of Pennsylvania did not support him, and he lost his post there. Jawaharlal Nehru, who knew and respected both him and his work, offered him a research post with the Indian government to do work on agricultural development problems in India, and he was engaged in that work. Alice was an able sociologist also working on Indian social problems, and they were living in Bombay with their young children. Dan and Alice were very insightful guides to my understanding of Indian society and its political economy, and they knew many of the leading Indian scholars in that field. They also very much enjoyed Indian music and art and the many cultural events taking place in Bombay and invited me to go with them. We remained good friends after we all left Bombay and saw each other in Paris where they later taught and lived, and Alice lives today, and in the United States where Alice has visited us after Dan's death.

Other close friends whom I met then were Gilbert Austin and his wife, Alice. Gilbert was the head of the USIA office in Bombay then, and later in Calcutta when I was there in 1962. He introduced me to several Indian journalists in Bombay. One of these, Nandan Kagal, became a good friend, as did his wife, Carmen, who was Gilbert's assistant in Bombay. Nandan was a very good guide to understanding intricacies of current events in India. Gilbert also put me in contact with American businessmen with interests in Bombay and thus with their experiences in the country. Gilbert and Alice and myself remained good friends long after we first met.

Another U.S. government officer, Bernard Zagorin, an economist in the American Embassy in New Delhi, was interested in my work and helpful in putting me in touch with useful contacts in the business world. We remained in touch subsequently, and Bernie was the person responsible for my being offered a post with the Asian Development Bank when it was established in 1966.

Apart from such academic, government, and other non-business people, in the course of my work and as part of it I met many of India's leading industrialists. Among these were J.R.D. Tata and G.D. Birla, who headed India's leading entrepreneurial families, controlling major firms in various industries. In Ahmedabad, which was India's major cotton textile industry center, I visited various textile factories and met and interviewed leading industrialists, including Kasturbhai Lalbhai, Surottam Hutheesingh and Vikram Sarabhai. I also visited the Tata Iron and Steel Co. (TISCO) factory in Jamshedpur, Bihar, which was the largest and most successful steel plant in India before the public sector plants were established. These private firms were all affected by government industrial policies restricting their growth and technological investment during the Plan periods of the 1950's and 1960's. In retrospect while overall industrial growth was stimulated by the Plans, the restrictive policies on private firms not only limited the private sector but also general longer term industrial growth. I also met various private sector economists. Tata's in Bombay had a major Economics Office associated with its headquarters, headed over time by two able economists, Y.S. Pandit in my earlier years and D.R. Pendse after 1972. The reports issued by this office, and my meetings with both these economists, were very helpful in understanding the changing role of the private sector in India's industrialization.

In those early years I was much impressed by the idealistic vision of the Indian political figures and economists whom I met. They were working for a better life for the Indian people and for a society that would be both fair in its treatment of different classes and castes and increasingly equitable in its results in terms of income and opportunities for all India's citizens. To help in achieving those goals by my research and for the better understanding of what was happening was very satisfying. I was struck too by the quality of the Indian bureaucracy and absence of corruption in getting things done at the time, especially in contrast to other South Asian countries – Philippines, Thailand and Indonesia – I worked in soon after. But I am struck today by how that characteristic has changed; corruption has reportedly become widespread at various levels of Indian society from the local to national. In my first stay in Bombay I also remember being caught in the great demonstrations for a Marathi language state and the underlying sense of violence in those demonstrations. This made me realize concretely the great achievement of Mahatma Gandhi in successfully creating a massive non-violent movement for independence in India. My observation of the underlying social and economic tensions in India aroused even more admiration for his achievements than I had before I had gone to India. And my respect for Jawaharlal Nehru's success in establishing an effective Indian democracy after 1947 is also very great.

During my first year, another American friend doing research in Bombay and I rented a car and drove from Bombay to Mysore in the south to see the then annual parade and celebration of the Maharajah's rule. (This no longer takes place.) We then drove via Kerala to the southern tip of India just above Ceylon and finally up the east coast to Madras, from where I took a train to return to Bombay. This and other trips gave me a sense of the size and variety of India, and of the pleasures of its mix of cultures and arts, the enjoyments of its festivities and of its different foods and physical beauties. India's sculptures, temples and palaces are among the greatest in the world – in Bombay the sculptured art of the Elephanta Caves; near Aurangabad, north of Bombay, the great Ellora and Ajanta Caves; the Buddhist sculptures of the north; Benares, the Holy City with its beautiful Hindu temples; the palaces in Delhi, the Taj Mahal in Agra, and the Mogul capital city of Fatehpur Sikri built by Akbar; and near Madras the Mahaballipuram temples. And as I have already mentioned, there was then, and is now, a very active contemporary art scene in all the large cities of India that I know.

There was then an active Indian film and literary life. In 1956 I saw in Bombay for the first time the great movie "Pather Pancheli" by Satyajit Ray, which I consider one of the best introductions to Indian society that I know; his trilogy of Apu movies, of which this is one, are among the greatest movies in film history. Today Indian films are among the most widely seen of any in the world. I read Indian literature written in English in Bombay for the first time – R.K. Narayan's short stories were a great introduction to the country. Tagore's poetry and fiction and his art I found very enjoyable; Nissim Ezekiel's and Dom Moraes' poetry were a pleasure to read, and there were many other authors. A bit later I read Salmon Rushdie's *Midnight's Children*, which I think is great, and have read his later books, as they have appeared; I have also read V.S. Naipaul's novels and non-fiction on India. They are very insightful on India's society, although I do not agree with all his ideas. On the basis of this experience I feel strongly that one of the best introductions to a developing country is its literature, since the country's novelists understand its society and how it works, and write well about it. For the teaching of economic development today I strongly recommend that the course begin with such a literary introduction to a developing country's life in its early economic stage to give students a picture of a developing society, whose process they will be studying and trying to understand.

One of the high points of that first year was an evening I spent on a roof of a home in Bombay overlooking the Indian Ocean, listening to the first concert I heard by Ravi Shankar on the sitar, with a group of other musicians. It began at about 8:00 or 9:00 P.M. and continued for many hours. The audience was enthralled, and the musicians did not play for a restricted time, but as the spirit moved them, improvising as they went along. It was a great experience. I've enjoyed Ravi Shankar's and others' sitar playing ever since, as well as broader Indian music. I also enjoyed then, and have since, Indian classic dance performances, and see those when I can.

Personally the most important event for me in that first year was that I married an Indian woman I met in Bombay. She was Kusum Parekh. Kusum was working for Indian Airlines in its Bombay office, and we met there. She came from Gujarat and her father, then already deceased, had been a supporter of Mahatma Gandhi and an associate of Jai Prakash Narayan, one of Mahatma Gandhi's followers as well as one of India's most progressive social thinkers and political leaders at the time. I wanted very much to get married and had been hoping to do that for some years. Kusum had a great deal of courage in accepting my offer. (As I have learned more about Indian society and the complexities of marriage among Indian families, I realize more the degree of her courage.) We were married in mid-1956, shortly before I was to return to the U.S., in a civil marriage in Bombay before a group of American friends, including the Thorners and Austins, several members of Kusum's family and our Indian friends. I had to return to the U.S. soon after the wedding. I found an apartment in Boston across the river from MIT, which was ready for Kusum when she arrived.

When she did arrive, I introduced her to my parents in Brooklyn and my family in Bridgeport and my cousins who were all living nearby. She was welcomed warmly, though I learned later that there had been some unhappiness among some of the older family that she was not Jewish, though all felt that, at age 36, it was about time that I had married. My mother also invited her friend, the poet Marianne Moore, for lunch to meet Kusum and me, and that was a pleasant occasion.

We settled in Boston, and Kusum became pregnant fairly soon after she arrived. She gave birth in 1957 to our son Mark Siddhartha (the Buddha's name) on November 14, the date of Nehru's Birthday. Kusum of course was busy with caring for our baby son. I helped to the extent I could, but I was busy with writing up my work of the previous year, preparing my next project in India and doing some part-time teaching at MIT. Kusum became accustomed to American living style, and we met socially various married MIT and Harvard graduate students and faculty interested in India. I still remember Kusum's pleasure in seeing her first snow in the 1956 winter in Boston, and the real beauty of the snow fronting our apartment. Kusum also then applied for, and became, a United States citizen.

I finished my first book on India's industrialization policies, *Industrial Change in India*, in late 1957. It was published in 1958 in the United States and 1959 in India. This work on capital requirements for industrial growth led me into the study of India's capital and financial markets. This became my second MIT Center project and led to my second year, 1958-1959, in Bombay, studying industrial finance in India. During those two interim years of preparation in Cambridge, there had been a change in the Center's India program. Bill Malenbaum left MIT to become Economics Professor at the University of Pennsylvania, concentrating on its India program. The new director of the MIT Center's India project was Paul Rosenstein-Rodan, who had headed its Italy project. The Center's South Italy and Indonesian projects had ended, and Ben Higgins had also left. Paul Rodan had taught many of India's leading economists in England before the war and independence, and had been a founder of the field of Economic Development in Economics. After the Center's first year of research in India, the Ford Foundation, very interested in India's development with Douglas Ensminger as its Resident Representative in Delhi, provided funding for continued research and policy assistance.

Terry Neale had left the Center India project after that first year, but we stayed in close touch and met often. Dick Eckaus was doing research on Indian economic issues using mathematical model analysis. Louis Lefeber had come from Latin America to MIT to write his Ph.D. there. With his past experience in Latin American development he had great interest in India's development issues and joined the India project. I was in regular contact with Dick and Louis on both a professional and, with Kusum, on a social level. I also was asked to talk to Paul Samuelson's seminar on my industrial finance project, and I talked about my work with Robert Solow and Charles Kindleberger who were both very interested in economic development issues, and of course Helen Lamb, who was still at the Center and a close friend. There were other economists and political scientists in Cambridge at MIT and Harvard working on various development issues in India and other Asian countries. At the MIT Center Everett Hagen was writing his pioneer work in Economic Development; in the political and social fields, Harold Isaacs, Jim Abgglen and Lucian Pye were doing major work on China, India and Japan, with Myron Weiner coming later with his work on India. At Harvard Edward Mason and Kenneth Galbraith were very much interested in South Asia; the Harvard Pakistan project was the center for many younger economists in the development policy field, who worked in Pakistan then and later in other major Asian developing countries, such as Indonesia. Albert Hirschman visited the MIT Center and Harvard periodically before joining the Harvard faulty. He was for me the most stimulating economist in the Economic Development field, with his breadth of approach in that whole area of study. There were also many younger visiting economists from India. These included Jagdish Bhagwati and Padma Desai living and teaching there, and if I remember rightly Amartya Sen and Sukhamoy Chakravarty were visiting research scholars. Two young American political scientists, Suzanne and Lloyd Rudolph, who had done major work in India were than at Harvard and associated with the MIT Center, and we became good friends. Our relationship has continued for many years after we had all left Cambridge and later lived in Chicago. It was a very lively atmosphere for the exchange of ideas on political economy issues with respect to Asia, on India and Pakistan primarily, but also on China, in which I had long been interested, and for my research. It was also a pleasant social atmosphere in which to introduce Kusum, whom my associates were interested in meeting.

We returned to India in June 1958 to start my industrial finance project in Bombay, and meet our Indian family and friends. Paul Rodan had established my formal connection with the Reserve Bank of India where my associate would be Dr. M. Narasimhan, a very able economist, whom I had met earlier. I was also of course in close touch with such former friends as Doctors K.S. Krishnaswamy, D. Khatkhate and V.V. Bhatt in the RBI.

In my second India year the MIT Center was more closely connected than previously with policy planning in the Planning Commission, reflecting both Paul Rodan's friendship with key economists on the Commission staff and the Ford Foundation interest. MIT had two senior economists in New Delhi, both leaders in the field of Economic growth analysis, Trevor Swan from the Australian National University and Ian Little from Oxford. They worked with the Perspective Planning Division of the Planning Commission, directed by Pitamber Pant, in preparing the Third Five Year Plan.

This time, instead of living in a small downtown Bombay apartment, I rented a house for Kusum, Mark and myself in a pleasant residential area, Worli Sea Face, some distance from downtown. I also rented a car and driver who could take me on my research related trips and take Kusum on the trips she needed to make. We were in close touch with Kusum's sister living in another part of town and with the many friends we had in Bombay. Kusum had family members in Gujarat, not far from Bombay, and we went there periodically.

My research went well. My previous work in India was well regarded. Through my friends at the RBI and other economists in Bombay and with my contacts among the industrialists I had met on my first visit I was able to meet many of India's leading financiers, government financial figures and borrowers in large and small enterprises to discuss the working of the industrial finance market and its problems. At Bombay University Doctors R.K. Hazari and L.C. Gupta were both doing research on industrial finance. We were good friends, and we met and exchanged ideas on our research. Sachin Chaudhuri published several of my articles on the research in "Economic Weekly," and these encouraged helpful comments from a wider audience.

The fact that two senior Center economists were working for the Planning Commission contributed to a greater interest in my work in New Delhi and I made several visits there to discuss my research with Planning Commission economists. Other foreign economists who might be visiting India and who were near Bombay also contacted me to discuss what I was doing. It was on such visits to Bombay that I first met Heinz Arndt from Australia, Michael Kidron and Paul Streeten from England, among others. We became good friends exchanging ideas and seeing each other after our first India meetings. During that year, Ian Little became one of my closest English friends. He and his wife, Dobs, visited Kusum and me, in Bombay. I think he has since done some of the most important work on Development Economics, and his teaching of Indian economists at Oxford may have had a significant influence upon India's longer term economic policy. He was a teacher there of Manmohan Singh, who became India's Finance Minister from 1991-1994, pursuing economic reform vigorously, and then Prime Minister after the 2004 elections, and of other Indian economists. Whenever I have visited England since we first met in 1958, I have tried to meet Ian.

That second year in Bombay was a good year. Personally, Kusum and I enjoyed ourselves watching Mark grow, being with family and friends, and taking advantage of Bombay's lively cultural and artistic activities. My research went well, and I gathered the material for my book and felt it might be of use for India's policy makers. We returned to MIT in the summer of 1959, living in a Cambridge apartment in 1959 to mid-1960. During that final year at MIT, I finished the book, based on the previous year's work, *Industrial Finance in India*, which was published in 1962 in the U.S. and India. It was an early volume on that subject then. During that year too I began work on my later, broader book on the political economy of India's development, which was finished and published in the mid-1960's when I was at RAND.

In 1985 I published a retrospective book, based on my Indian experience on the MIT Center Project in India and on my knowledge of the Harvard Pakistan project during many of the same years. I write about the writing of that book in a later chapter since I wrote it twenty years after. I wrote it because I thought my past experiences were relevant to the broader issues of the role of foreign advisors in countries going through economic policy changes then; I think that is even more so today.

B. After MIT: Our return to India via Nepal

I left MIT in 1965 when my work with the Center project ended, to join the United Nations as an economist with the Industry Division of its Economics Office, based at the U.N.'s New York Headquarters. Kusum and I and Mark moved to New York, finding an apartment not far from Greenwich Village and an easy subway ride to the U.N. We had close family in Brooklyn, and Bridgeport was fifty miles away, but resettling could not have been easy for Kusum. But New York is a city with much to do, and Indian restaurants were beginning to open up; though I remember that there was only one Indian restaurant then near the U.N. There were Indian professional staff members, including economists, at Headquarters, and I met some of these. We became friends, which also made the move easier for Kusum.

However, it turned out that my work was not very interesting. While I met such able senior economists as Hans Singer and Sam Lurie, who headed the division in which I worked, the work itself was more bureaucratic, report-writing and paper shuffling in preparing periodic reports on world industrialization. The interesting work for the U.N. was working overseas in U.N. offices in developing countries or in its aid work in such countries. I was not doing that, and I began exploring other possibilities.

In 1961 I was approached by the Ford Foundation to become an advisor on economic planning to the Nepalese government. A democratic government had been elected in Nepal, and the Ford Foundation Office in India, headed by Douglas Ensminger, had been asked by that government, and negotiated an agreement with it, to provide a group of advisors. That had actually been negotiated by Wolf Ladejinsky, the agricultural economist who had played an important role among American advisors on agricultural policy in Japan and Korea, and whom I knew well. Soon after that agreement had been signed, the King of Nepal dismissed that government and assumed governing power himself, but he asked the Ford Foundation to continue the agreement and provide advisors. I was then asked by Ford if I would be willing to go for a two year term, and I accepted. Another young economist, William Thweatt, with past experience in Latin America, also accepted.

Kusum and I left the United States for Nepal after New Year's 1961. I remember I was asked to bring formal wear since that would be necessary if I were to meet the King. En route to Nepal I first went to Pakistan to discuss advisory methods and issues with Harvard advisors in that country and then went to Delhi to talk with Doug Ensminger about the Nepal project and to learn something of Nepal itself and its relations to India. Kusum and Mark had flown directly to Bombay to visit with her family before Nepal, and I joined them briefly before we all went north.

A road from Kathmandu, Nepal's capital, had only been completed in the mid-1950's, opening it up to India. Commercial air transportation was available, but the passenger planes were still two-engine propeller planes, and during the monsoon season and heavy winter snow air flights were frequently down for extended periods. Thus the country was still not the tourist haven it would become in the late 1960's. It was a beautiful mountain land, with little smog and lovely views of the Himalayas from Kathmandu and Pokhara in the west. It was also almost an entirely agricultural economy, self-sufficient in food, but generally at a low income level. There was a demand for higher income through economic growth and for social improvement. There was significant political influence of ideas from India for political democracy and socialism. Some Nepali had been educated there before and after India's independence, and others had worked there, including the Gurkhas enrolled in the English army stationed in India. There was also significant influence from China, its northern neighbor, with its Communist government and economic policy. The Nepal Government's major interest was to maintain its political independence and security between those two great neighbors – India to its south and China to its north. It sought to balance potential excess power from one country by using the other as a counter-balance, and to use influence from international agencies and other countries, such as the United States and Scandinavian countries, as a third influence to balance both great neighbors. Maintaining its own independence was its major policy goal, as it always had been.

When Bill Thweatt and I arrived, shortly after King Mahendra had taken over power, the government was in disarray, and the machinery for economic policy-making for development had not been established. After some months, Bekh Bahardur Thapa returned from economic study in the United States to become the major Economic Officer in the Planning Agency; then economic policy-making began and we started our advisory work.

In that interval between our arrival and Bekh Thapa's return from the United States, Kusum and I enjoyed the beautiful country. We had a pleasant home in Kathmandu and the use of a car and driver, which were necessary. I was able to do whatever work I had to do, establishing contacts with various economic officers in the government, talking with knowledgeable foreigners from the United States, India and various mountainous European countries such as Sweden and Norway, meeting businessmen in the city and getting a sense, by travel, of life and economic activity in valleys other than Kathmandu. I was struck by Nepal's role with respect to India's trade. With the Indian government's tight restrictions on import to, and exports from India, Nepal became a channel for smuggled imports to and exports from India, to third countries. Trade to and from the third countries to Nepal was relatively free as far as Nepal was concerned. Smuggling to and from India via Nepal was possible, and not difficult, for Indian businessmen with good connections who were thus able to bypass those controls. I don't think it was very large in monetary terms as far as India was concerned, though no data were available, but stories of that trade were common.

I wore my formal dress on only one occasion. Queen Elizabeth of England and the Duke of Edinburgh visited Nepal during our time there. There was a large formal reception for them to which Kusum and I and other foreigners were invited, and we actually met the Queen herself and exchanged a few polite remarks. An interesting by-product of the Queen's visit was that many of the roads in, to, and near, Kathmandu on which she might ride were repaired, some street lights were installed, and electric power was expanded in the city before she arrived – positive development effect to impress the Queen. There was a negative cultural by-product. An impressive Hindu temple in the city contained some lovely nude sculptures that it was feared the Queen might consider erotic. The bodies of those figures were covered before that visit, probably to avoid offending the Queen. The Queen's visit of course was only an incidental bypass to our time there, but it was an interesting one in cultural terms, and the only personal contact I have ever had with royalty. Our work in Nepal ended after only about nine months in the Fall of 1961. The reason for the early end was that the Ford Foundation had just agreed to provide assistance to the West Bengal Government to prepare a Plan for Calcutta's future development, and I was shifted to Calcutta to serve as economist on that project. I had a good knowledge of India's economy from my MIT work, and was not doing much economic advisory work in Nepal on that project. Bill Thweatt remained there after I left.

I enjoyed the time in Nepal, as did Kusum and, I expect, our four-year-old son. It was a beautiful country, not yet overrun by tourists or smog as its opening accelerated. I returned again about thirty years later for a week at Christmas, and there had been a great change. Kathmandu, where I visited, was greatly changed with far more traffic. I and my wife were besieged by sellers on the streets, and bargaining was intense. The smog was very heavy, and it was not possible to see the Himalayas during the daytime. Many of the temples were also no longer open to individual visitors, which was a real personal loss. I no longer knew anything of the economy; the income gains to businessmen in Kathmandu dealing with the large number of tourists may have been high, but I wondered whether the farmers had benefited from the changes.

My experience in Calcutta after we got there in late 1961 was much different from that in Nepal. The work on the Calcutta plan project was full-time and very interesting. That plan preparation was triggered by the West Bengal and Indian governments' request for a World Bank loan to build a second bridge across the Hooghly River. While such a bridge seemed necessary, there was no plan for the city's future development, or its relation to Northeast India, and the relevance of the new bridge to that future. The World Bank made the preparation of such a plan a prerequisite for a loan for that second bridge. The Ford Foundation, which had provided assistance for the earlier preparation of a very useful plan for New Delhi, was asked by the Government to do the same for Calcutta. The West Bengal Government established the Calcutta Metropolitan Planning Organization (the CMPO) to prepare that plan, and the Ford Foundation team was advisory to the CMPO.

Before I moved to Calcutta to work, I had visited the city a few times, but largely as a tourist. In my first brief visit in 1952 I had stayed at the Great Eastern Hotel in the center of the city and had been struck by the numerous beggars and apparent pervasive poverty. When I was with the MIT Center in Bombay, I had gone once or twice to the Indian Statistical Institute (the ISI) outside of Calcutta, meeting Professor Mahalanobis and some of the economists there and at the university, but I had little sense of the city and region. From my Bombay years my close friendship with Sachin Chaudhuri, and some of the Bengali economists who were his friends, turned out to be an ideal introduction for my later residence and work in Calcutta from about the Fall of 1961 to November 1962. During that year, Kusum and Mark and I lived in a rented home in an upscale neighborhood in Calcutta, and we had a rented car and driver. The house was not very distant by car from the CMPO offices where I had space, office facilities and close contact with both my Indian counterparts in, and other Ford Foundation advisors to, the CMPO.

In the course of my work I met many of the leading businessmen in Calcutta, which had been one of India's major economic and industrial centers in the pre-independence United India. It had been the center of the jute textile industry with jute grown in East Bengal manufactured into cloth in Calcutta. Several large iron and steel plants were operating near Calcutta manufacturing products from iron and coal mines in nearby areas. One of these was the Tata Iron and Steel (TISCO) plant in Bihar, the largest then in India, with its business offices in Calcutta itself. There was a large and successful Marwari business community also operating in and from Calcutta, with the Birla family headquarters there. The city had been the British capital of India until the early Twentieth Century before the capital was moved to Delhi. This position had made Calcutta a major administrative center and contributed to its economic and social leadership which had continued even after the capital had moved. Its location on the Hooghly River, leading into the Bay of Bengal, led to its becoming a major national seaport. It had been the center of India's intellectual life before independence, with the great novelist, and Nobel Prize winner, Rabindranath Tagore representative of that leadership. It was a major non-Gandhian center of the pre-war independence movement under Subash Chandra Bose, who had left India in the Second World War to fight with the Japanese against the British. Calcutta University was one of India's academic centers and the ISI a leading economic research center, whose Director, P.C. Mahalanobis, had been Nehru's fellow student in England and was a major influence on India's post-war planning. The Communist Party in the state was strong politically and a challenge to the state's governing Congress Party. One of the hoped for by-products of a Calcutta Plan and the building of the Second Bridge would be strengthening of the state's Congress Party's ability to continue to defeat the Communist Party in the state.

The development of the plan for Calcutta was a challenge. The partition of Bengal after independence had weakened Calcutta's economy with the jute textile industry hard hit by loss of its internal raw material source to Pakistan. India's foreign trade fell significantly after the war and independence, and the high restrictions on foreign trade hurt Calcutta as a port. Steel and machinery production were also negatively affected by the price and output controls on metal products manufacture. In my research I sought to understand those problems, how they affected Calcutta's future economic role in the region, future trade within and without the region, and the regional transportation needs, including a Second Bridge. Another significant research interest was the possible development of a second port, Haldia, on the Bay of Bengal itself, and provision of appropriate transportation between Calcutta and Haldia. It was hoped too that successful growth of the Calcutta area would have a wider positive effect on the state's rural sector and that of the neighboring East Indian states, Orissa and Bihar. It was an interesting year of research not only on specific economic issues, but broader socio-political questions. I wrote several reports on the economic problems I was working on and made suggestions for actions relevant for development and future transport requirements, including the Hooghly Bridge.

In my work I got to know both American colleagues with whom I worked and Indian counterparts on the CMPO staff. Among the former, Jack Carroll and his wife, Marion, became life-time friends. Jack was, like myself, a senior project economist and Marion was the project librarian. Two other economists there with whom I briefly overlapped were Stan Wellisz who had been at MIT, and Bill Vickery visiting briefly from Columbia University.

The Indian economist on the project itself whom I knew best was Lalita Chakravarty, the wife of Sukhamoy Chakravarty, then at Delhi University while she lived in Calcutta. They became close personal friends and we remained such long after I left Calcutta. I strengthened my friendship with Ashok Mitra, then at the ISI, and with Harendra Mazumdar, also there. They both became lifetime friends whom I still see when I go to Calcutta. I also developed both a professional relationship and close personal friendship until his death with Asok Mitra, at the time India's Census Commissioner in charge of preparing and publishing the 1960 Census. He not only provided essential information on economic and population trends in the area, but was a very knowledgeable guide to Bengal history and society. I think his later autobiography is an excellent guide to both that history and to Indian-British relations before Independence when he had been appointed to the Indian Civil Service. Amartya Sen was then in Delhi, and we met every so often there or on his visits to Calcutta.

Apart from my work itself, but flowing from it and from my friendships with my co-workers and with Sachin Chaudhuri and other Bengali friends, I learned how great a city Calcutta was culturally and intellectually. It was one of the most stimulating experiences I have had. I read Bengali literature written in the past and being written then that was widely discussed. I saw works by the many artists who had worked there in the past and contemporary artists working there now, and went to the continuous music, dance and theatre being performed. This all made the city very exciting. In a broad cultural sense Calcutta was close to the New York I knew in the 1930's and 1940's and the excitement I felt there then. I had felt some of that in Bombay in my two years there in the late 1950's, but it was greater in Calcutta. For an American or other western visitor this is an unusual view of Calcutta, and I don't know whether I would have the same feeling in 2004, only having been back there for short visits since 1963. But I recently read an article in the April 18, 2004 "Washington Post", p. F1 by a contemporary American author, John Augard, who had visited Calcutta stressing that same quality. Most of the American and European impressions of Calcutta, even by such a major writer as Gunther Grass, as well as others published in the past forty years, have stressed the poverty of the people there, within a Mother Theresa type vision. I think that the poverty is clearly true; Mother Theresa has done great work in creating awareness of and dealing with that poverty and her work must be supported. But the city's stimulating quality and its greatness as a world cultural center is generally unknown and neglected.

My contract with Ford ended in late 1962. I could have renewed it for another two years, but I was then offered a longer term economist post with the RAND Corporation in Los Angeles. RAND is a major U.S. policy oriented research organization then funded by the Defense Department but doing research on broader international policy issues not only directly related to defense. One of the top American economists in the development field in 1962 was a RAND economist, Charles Wolf, who had studied at Harvard, worked there on economic development problems and with the Harvard Pakistan Project under

Ed Mason before joining RAND. I had gotten to know him, and thought highly of his work, when I had been at the MIT Center in Cambridge and India. In 1962 RAND decided to begin continued study of longer term political-economy issues in India and South Asia and their implications for U.S. policy in Asia. Charlie Wolf knew my work and suggested to the Director of RAND's Economic Department that he offer me a post, which he did, and I accepted. I moved back to the United States with Kusum and Mark in October 1962, stopping briefly en route in Bombay to see Kusum's family there. Then we went to New York to see my mother and father, who were still living in Brooklyn and running their store, and to Bridgeport to see family there before going on to Los Angeles to settle in what was an entirely new location for all of us.

As a post-script, while I gained a great deal from my Calcutta year in terms of understanding a wider Indian culture, as well as its economy, the urban planning project I worked on did not have a short-term effect. As far as I know the Plan that we were working on was not completed. I've never seen a published copy. Eventually a Second Hooghly River Bridge was built, but not resulting from the Ford assisted CMPO work. One of the projects being studied then was an elevated rail system; it was felt an underground system would be too difficult since the water level under Calcutta was so high. The hoped for political effect of the CMPO project also did not result. The Congress Party was defeated in the state elections in the later 1960's. The Communist Party was the elected state governing party, has won repeated re-elections and governed West Bengal since. Under that party's government, with Russian aid, an underground city subway system was constructed and has been operating well for many years. A Second Hooghly Bridge was also eventually built. I have yet to see any study of the record of the democratically elected Communist Party government in West Bengal in terms of its economic and social achievements in the state. That would be very interesting, especially if it were combined with a study of the experience in Kerala State where another state Communist Party governed for many years. I hope I'll be alive to read such a book fairly soon.

CHAPTER VI

With RAND Living in California and Working on India and South Asia

M Y WORK AT RAND was at first to do research on the changing political-economic situation in India primarily, but if needed in the wider South Asia region, and its implications for American policy in Asia. In that respect it was an extension of my work with the State Department on Japan a decade earlier, but of another part of Asia, and in a longer term perspective rather than on short-term issues. RAND's function was work on longer term issues for the Defense Department.

The first work I did at RAND therefore was to finish my manuscript that I had started at MIT on the Indian political-economic framework and its future trends. My later experience in Calcutta led to the final version, which was finished in 1964 and accepted by the University of California Press the next year as a RAND publication. That book, *Democracy and Economic Change in India*, was one of the first American post-Indian independence books on that subject, and was widely read in South Asian academic courses and by a wider audience interested in India. I have been told by many people I have met since then that they read it when they were students. The first edition of 1966 was followed by a somewhat revised paperback edition in 1967, the revisions arising from some of the changes in 1966. I think that has been the most widely read of any of the books I've written with the largest sales. However, I received no royalties from those sales, because as a RAND publication, its royalties went to RAND. If I had remained with RAND my annual salary increases would have reflected those royalties, but I left RAND before royalties began. One of the key themes of the book was the rapid decline of caste and communal factors in political and economic policy-making on a national basis, and the growing importance of class and income forces. Over a forty years hindsight I think this has been occurring, but more gradually and in a more complex interrelated fashion than I had anticipated. But India is an effective democracy, and the most recent 2004 national election clearly confirms that. A fundamentalist religious government was defeated by a popular vote despite apparent economic successes because it did not extend the benefits of that economic growth to the wider public, and it was replaced by a secular government. Other significant political changes occurred at the state level as well as the national, and it will be very interesting to see what the new governments will accomplish. Such changes could not occur in China or Pakistan today.

RAND itself was a very interesting place to work at in the 1960's. Charlie Wolf was doing major work on Asian growth issues and broader development problems, and he became director of RAND's graduate level public policy analysis program when that began in the late 1960's. Albert Wohlstetter was a major thinker in the political field on the changing international scene and America's future role. I did not agree with some of his ideas, but they were always stimulating and provocative. His wife, Roberta, wrote the best book I have read on Pearl Harbor. At that time also James Schlesinger, Daniel Ellsberg and Nancy Nimitz were working for RAND. I thought their ideas were very insightful on international policy issues, both political and economic, and American policy. The economist who was most stimulating for my economic thinking was Richard Nelson, carrying out his path-breaking work on the importance of technological change for economic growth, and appropriate policy to stimulate technological change. I had always considered Joseph Schumpeter's writing in that field some of the most important economic work of the Twentieth Century. Dick Nelson is a worthy successor to Schumpeter. I regard his work among the most significant in contemporary Economics. It has strongly influenced my own thinking on economic policy for growth in developing countries, and on recent visits to India I have spoken on the desirability of policies to stimulate technological change in India and to spread resulting benefits. Burt Klein, who headed RAND's Economic Division for part of the time I was there, also did major work in that field. Francis Shieh was also an economist, originally from China, who was working on the Chinese economy for RAND then. We became good friends and have remained in touch after we both left RAND for other positions, including academic careers.

Apart from the people I met at RAND itself, the University of California at Los Angeles (UCLA) campus was near RAND and where we lived. There was close contact between academics there and RAND staff exchanging ideas and relevant experience. John Hitchcock, a leading anthropologist on Nepal, was there. We first met then, and our friendship continued after he had moved to the University of Wisconsin at Madison and I to the University of Illinois at Chicago. Among UCLA economists I met Armin Alchian and Jack Hirschleifer at various meetings, and we exchanged ideas on work in progress. Through a UCLA friend I also met Eliezer Ayal, then at the Berkeley University of California campus, before I went to Thailand for RAND, and his suggestions were very helpful for my work there. When I came to the University of Illinois at Chicago in 1972, he was on the Economics faculty there, and we became good friends.

I had voted for John F. Kennedy for President in the 1960 elections before going to Nepal. In the almost three years before his assassination in November 1963, he was responsible for the United States playing a greater role in the whole economic development area, using economic aid as a major U.S. growth supporting policy in the developing countries of Asia especially. Chester Bowles, who had been American Ambassador to India, was appointed Under-Secretary of State, Kenneth Galbraith American Ambassador to India, and Walt Rostow appointed a top White House Advisor. Max Millikan became an important external advisor to the administration. An effect of this was both greater direct U.S. aid to South Asian countries and greater support of the World Bank's work in the region.

A major force behind this interest in Asia, apart from the aim of improved general well-being there, was the fear of Communist expansion and of China's presumed threat in particular. India was regarded as a model, of growth by democratic means, counter to that of Communist China, but apart from being an economic example China was the strongest military power among the developing Asian countries. Chinese support for North Korea had contributed to the Korean War in the 1950's, and to the Two Koreas after it ended. After Vietnam had won post-World War II independence from France, there was communist rule in the north and its threatened expansion to the south; Indonesia too had a strong communist movement after independence from the Dutch, and from Japan following the war. While Thailand had been independent there was a fear of communism there, as well as in other neighbors of Vietnam, if communists won in Vietnam. RAND's policy analysis was associated with that direction in our policy, supporting democracy where it existed, as in India, and promoting a democratic alternative to an authoritarian state in other countries where such an alternative might exist and seemed feasible. (The MIT Center's work in India and Indonesia had been stimulated by that same issue.)

The most dramatic event I recall at RAND during 1963, my first year there, was hearing the news of President Kennedy's murder in November, while I was eating lunch at RAND, repeating my experience of learning of Pearl Harbor at lunch at Princeton. I still recall my sadness at seeing the TV photos of Jacqueline Kennedy and her children during the funeral, and my admiration for the courage she showed then. Lyndon Johnson, who became President, extended and strengthened President Kennedy's economic and social policies, including black and white integration policies within the United States, and maintained the earlier international economic development and anti-communist policies. These policies in Southeast Asia led to a more intensive American commitment in Vietnam and stronger resistance to a Communist North Vietnam takeover of South Vietnam, and eventually to the Vietnam War. Recently questions have been raised as to whether President Kennedy would have engaged the United States in that war, but no definitive answer seems to have been reached. Before the Vietnam War itself began, Southeast Asia had become a major area for American policy in Asia. The primary emphasis of my RAND work therefore shifted from India, where it had been focused through 1964 and included several short visits there, to Southeast Asia.

In 1965 I went to Thailand for almost a year to examine that country's economic problems and suggest appropriate American policy to ensure its economic well-being and development. I went with Kusum and Mark to Bangkok for that time. We had a pleasant place to live and transportation was easily available. Mark, then seven years old, went to an English language school that he liked and Kusum enjoyed the city with its Buddhist temples and various historical sites. It was still "The Venice of the Orient" with its internal canal system.

My work kept me busy. I met various senior Thai government economic officials, Thai academic economists knowledgeable of the Thai economic problems, local industrialists and other businessmen both in and out of Bangkok itself, and foreign investors. With all of these I discussed the country's problems and economic policies and their opinions as to those policies. Among the economists I then met were two who had degrees from American Universities, Dr. Snoh Unakul and Dr. Amnuey Viravan. Both were able and very helpful in my research with their knowledge of the Thai economy. We were friends and I saw Dr. Viravan and his wife again years later when I returned to Bangkok for an academic conference, and he had become a major political figure there. My work also took me to other parts of the country to examine the rural economy and the condition of the farm population to a limited extent since I did not know the language or much of agricultural economic issues. But as in India, the bulk of the Thai people are in agriculture, on which the economy relies heavily, and I felt I should have some sense of problems in that sector as well as industry and commerce. I was struck too by the role of overseas Chinese migrants in the Thai economy and society and how they had been successfully integrated and accepted in the country. This may have resulted in part from Thailand's continued independence – it has never been a colony – and the resulting mutual respect of the two peoples for each other and their mutual confidence, rather than fear or differences. Harry Barnes was the American Ambassador to Thailand at that time, if I remember rightly, and I was in contact with him. I thought very highly of him for his sensitivity to the Thai role in the region. I was very glad to renew my acquaintance with him later when he had become Ambassador to India and I was doing academic research there.

Apart from work we enjoyed the city, which had within and near it attractive and interesting religious and historical centers, temples and palaces containing beautiful art – sculptures, paintings and tapestries. Thai music and dance were enjoyable. I wish there was more available in Chicago, and I liked Thai food there, especially dishes with coconut and Thai fruits. Fortunately Thai restaurants are now quite numerous in the U.S., and I can get some of these foods here. The fact that Bangkok is near the sea made it possible to get away for a pleasant weekend during the hot months to Pattaya and other small towns on the water that were not then crowded with tourists. A country I also very much enjoyed visiting was nearby Cambodia, then governed by a friendly ruler, with its great Angkor Wat temple and palace ruins. They are one of the great monuments of Asia and world civilization, and their rediscovery by French archeologists a major cultural contribution – and we were very glad we were able to visit them while they were still in good shape. I was fortunately able to visit there again when I was working in Manila between 1967 and 1972. It has only been in very recent years that Cambodia is once again open after the isolation of the Pol Pot regime and friends have visited Angkor Wat. Thus, we enjoyed Bangkok a good deal, although it was not as stimulating intellectually or artistically in a contemporary sense as Bombay and Calcutta, but it did not have the obvious poverty that India showed. It was also not a democracy then and was not as politically interesting with various parties and campaigns, but it was a stable and peaceful benevolent despotism and eventually moved to a more democratic royal government.

I visited Bangkok again in the late 1990's for an economic conference at one of the universities there. The state has become more democratic in its government under the royal family, and there was more open political exchange with elections. The economy had done well and the city was prosperous, but now it was a sprawling urban mass. Crossing a main street was a real risk – a few years earlier Elie Ayal had been injured by a bus while waiting to cross – and I was warned to only cross on a fly-over. The old canal had disappeared and auto traffic was fierce. The nearby beach areas had become massive tourist centers with giant hotels, in part as a result of visits from American troops on leave from military service in Vietnam.

On the basis of that time in Thailand I wrote my report, and on my return to RAND and the United States went to Washington to brief the then responsible Assistant Secretary of Defense for Southeast Asia on my observations and recommendations on U.S. policy with respect to Thailand's economy. Soon after that report, I went to Taiwan in 1965 with Charlie Wolf and another colleague on a short mission to look at economic issues there and American policies related to Taiwan's economic growth and its relationship to mainland Communist China. During our short time there, we were impressed by Taiwan's apparently prosperous economic condition when compared to its other developing country neighbors, and the Taiwanese policies supporting that growth. A successful land reform program had been introduced with American support with the advisory assistance of Wolf Ladejinsky, who had played such a major role in introducing the Japanese land reform. This land reform had significantly stimulated broader economic growth in Taiwan, and built broader local support for Chiang Kai Shek's government there. It was enjoyable also to visit some of the attractive rural areas outside of Taipei. The Taipei Museum, which had one of the world's great collections of Chinese art, was a great pleasure. Many of its works had been removed from the Peking Museum and shipped to Taiwan when Chiang Kai Shek fled Beijing.

While at RAND, I was asked by the World Bank to serve on the Bank's first mission to Afghanistan in 1965 as its industrial economist. The mission head was Orville McDiarmid, whom I had known from Japan and his later Bank work in India. The mission report was to examine Afghanistan's current economic situation and recommend both a set of national policies to stimulate growth, and a World Bank aid program to support those policies in agriculture and industry. We were in Afghanistan for about three months, during which time I was away from my family.

My time in Afghanistan was a most interesting experience. Nepal was the one country I knew to which Afghanistan was comparable, both mountainous and landlocked. But geographically Afghanistan was much larger with much wider valleys and numerous mountains, although not as high as the Himalayas. Nepal had to balance its independence between two giant neighbors, India and China. Afghanistan had for centuries maintained independence despite threats and attacks from Tsarist Russia and imperial Great Britain, which feared attacks on India from Russia via Afghanistan. After the Second World War there was fear of attack from Communist Russia and non-communist American friends. Furthermore, like Nepal, each valley had its own dominant ruling group with the country as a whole unified under the rule of the royal family. International support from the United Nations and such international aid agencies as the World Bank was seen as contributing to Afghanistan's political independence. Economic growth and rising family income were means of strengthening support across local loyalties for the national government. The United States also supported the Afghan request for a World Bank mission and aid from the Bank to resist Russian influence there.

My mission work was to examine the country's industrial structure and its industrial prospects. My actual research was largely restricted to the northern and central areas which the royal government controlled; I did not visit the pro-communist regions although nominally they were under the royal government. I traveled to those northern and central regions, generally not far from Pakistan, visiting factories and talking to government officials and businessmen operating in those regions of the country, as well as to national officials. I accomplished my assignment and liked the work very much. The Afghans I spoke to, some educated in the United States and Europe, were interested in, and helpful for, my work, hoping it would benefit the country. I wrote my report and it was part of the larger one. It was a guide to World Bank policy toward the country and was useful to the Afghan governing officials. Unfortunately, when a later Russian inspired rebellion overthrew the government, the country went through an extended civil war resulting eventually in an American supported Taliban religious fundamentalist government in the recent years before 2001. During that entire period economic development policy was quite forgotten.

A great added pleasure was the beauty of the country's mountain and valley landscape. Afghanistan too had been a major section of the "Great Silk Road," going back to ancient Greek and Roman history, for the land trade between Europe and Asia to China, which continued through the 18th and 19th Centuries before the Suez Canal was built. Along the Afghan section of the Silk Road there were still sculptures and ruins going back to the Alexandrian Gandhara period. Afghanistan had also been a center of Buddhism before Muslim rule and the Bayon Statues outside of Kabul were a monument to Buddhism that had been preserved through history. The Kabul Museum was a world class museum with a great collection of Afghan art throughout the country's history. The recent news items I have seen that the Taliban government destroyed the Bayon statues and closed the museum, many of whose works may have been stolen or smashed, is a significant cultural loss on a world scale.

From my little knowledge of Afghanistan today this is apparently a time of great uncertainty there. After September 11, 2001, the Taliban, which supported Osama Bin Laden's terrorism, was forced from power. But the United States and United Nations have not yet established a stable successor national secular government. I hope the United Nations will take the lead in doing this, with American and European support. The American government and public should recognize that this will be a long-term effort. Results will not be very rapid or spectacular. Success in the policy goal requires a good knowledge of a complex country and society, with many differing regions and social groups. I believe an important element of such a program should be not to repeat our support of a fundamentalist religious group for political leadership. We must also recognize that establishing a stable secular government will require long-term economic aid and probably significant military support to ensure successful and peaceful transition.

I returned from Afghanistan to RAND and my work there by mid-1966. Soon after I learned that my contract would not be continued after 1967. India had declined in importance as far as American policy was concerned, as Vietnam and Southeast Asia became more important, and there was less need felt for India economic expertise at RAND. My four years there had been both productive and stimulating for me. Apart from publishing a major book on India's political economy I had also learned about other countries of Asia than those in which I had previously worked. The professional staff at RAND had been very stimulating in terms of exchange of ideas, and I gained much from that interchange. I benefited further by having to write, as in the State Department, for policy-makers rather than a highly restricted academic audience. My writing was in a language for the educated decision-maker, and not in the mathematical jargon that so much of economic writing had become. I enjoyed that, but I learned later it would not help me return to what academic Economics had become since I had left it in the 1950's.

During the 1960's, the Indian economy and polity had gone through significant changes. In the early '60's there had been serious economic problems; in the mid-'60's India had suffered a significant military defeat by China over northeast border issues, and this contributed to reduced political importance for the United States; Prime Minister Nehru, a founding father of the new state and a world figure died. The transition to his successor was peaceful, but Lal Bahadur Shastri did not have his stature, though he was highly respected while Prime Minister, and he died after only a few years in that post. Pakistan had been defeated by India in war and had gone through major government changes during the decade. Both of these area changes led to a decline in American interest in South Asia. In Vietnam the non-communist South Vietnam government had been greatly weakened, and North Vietnamese efforts to overthrow it seemed near success. Lyndon Johnson considered it crucial for the U.S. to prevent that overthrow; the continued expansion of Communism in Asia would be very difficult to resist if it occurred. There was a major increase of U.S. military support for South Vietnam and the Vietnam War became a reality. RAND consultants, including Dan Ellsberg and Jim Schlesinger, provided advice at this early stage of the war. I supported it at the time, remembering the Korean War that had maintained an independent non-communist South Korea, and aware of the threat China now seemed to pose to India after their years of peace and friendly relations had ended. However, I was also wondering if there were not peaceful methods to prevent communist expansion given the high costs of war and its resulting destruction. I strongly supported added assistance for economic development in Asia, and associated efforts for social improvement and adjustment programs such as land reform, educational expansion, social welfare and income redistribution. While I lost contact with my former RAND colleagues other than Charlie Wolf and Dick Nelson after 1967, I have read Dan Ellsberg's book on his change in viewpoint towards the Vietnam War and his actions resulting from that change, and I admire his courage. I have also read Robert MacNamara's recent book on his growing disagreement with President Johnson on Vietnam. I was particularly struck in both their accounts of how little the American decision-makers knew of Vietnam when they were making those decisions. I am worried that we may have repeated similar ignorance-based decisions in Afghanistan, where we supported the religious fundamentalist Taliban for many years before September 11, 2001, and in Iraq after that attack. Saddam Hussein had been our main ally against Iran in the 1980's before he attacked Kuwait, though he was an oppressive dictator, and we apparently overthrew him on the basis of very inaccurate reports. In both Afghanistan and Iraq we are currently trying to form successor governments to the Taliban and Hussein. Those experiences in regions where I had some experience worry me that we may be making similar errors, in part from lack of knowledge, with respect to our relations with countries in other parts of the world as well.

In late 1966 I received an offer for a senior economic position with the newly established Asian Development Bank (ADB). The ADB was set up as a regional development bank, modeled on the Inter-American Development Bank, to provide economic support to the non-communist Asian countries. It was to be financed by funding from the developed Asian and non-Asian countries with an interest in economic development of the poorest Asian countries. Japan had been a prime force behind its establishment. United States support came later, in part motivated to show that we had broader interests in Asia than simply fighting communism by war, and we supported significant economic aid to the entire continent. With the commitment of American funding and political support the Bank was eventually established with its headquarters in Manila, capitol of the Philippines, a developing country not dominated economically by Japan and now politically independent from the United States.

Bernard Zagorin, whom I had known for many years while we were both in India, had played a major role in the U.S. State Department's work to establish the ADB. He was the first American representative on the ADB's Board. He asked me if I would be interested in an appointment on the Bank's staff. When I told him I would be interested, he gave my name to Takeshi Watanabe, the ADB's first President, who had been a former top official of the Japanese Finance Ministry and Japan's representative on the World Bank's Board. I had lunch with Mr. Watanabe and his assistant, Toyo Gyohten, during a visit they were making to the United States. It was a very pleasant meeting. It turned out that I had met Mr. Watanabe when I had been working on Japan for the State Department in the early 1950's, and Toyo Gyohten had been a scholar in the Princeton Graduate College Economics Department in the late 1950's. Soon after our lunch I was offered a senior position on the ADB staff, effective after I came to Manila in late 1966. After talking with Kusum I accepted the offer, and we made our plans to leave Los Angeles after Mark's school term ended. Meanwhile I wound up my RAND work, we packed what we would bring to Manila, and put our house on the market. I myself left Los Angeles at the end of 1966 to begin work in Manila, and Kusum and Mark joined me a month later after I found an apartment in Manila.

While my new job looked very promising, we were sorry to leave Los Angeles. We had become settled in an attractive home near UCLA, had good friends at RAND, UCLA and among Indian-Americans living in the area, and Mark liked his school. Los Angeles itself, without a downtown and with its sprawling road system, was not as attractive as New York or San Francisco in a stimulating cultural sense. It had, however, the great attractiveness of being within easy driving distance of ocean, mountain and desert areas, and we enjoyed all three of them. But RAND had ended for me, and the ADB seemed very engaging as a challenging opportunity.

Apart form the attractiveness of Los Angeles itself I have another retrospective comment on the broader Californian political atmosphere at the time, which I did not find attractive. This was before the 1968 experience which I did not have. But when I was there I was struck by the intensity of political attitudes in that state, especially on the part of the state Republican Party then led by Richard Nixon, who had been California Senator and Vice-President from 1952 to 1960, and by Ronald Reagan. California had a liberal Democratic governor for some years in the 1950's and 1960's. That administration had introduced significant social benefits within the state. Among these was the major expansion of the University of California system, especially at Berkeley and Los Angeles, which had become two of America's leading campuses, but also elsewhere, headed by a very able progressive labor economist, Clark Kerr. The Democratic Party was defeated in the state when Ronald Reagan ran for governor and won a mid-1960's election after an extremely partisan campaign. One of his first actions after taking office was to dismiss Clark Kerr as University President on purely partisan grounds. I think this was a preliminary trigger, among others, to the extremities of the later 1960's and 1968. The degree of extremity and intemperance was far greater than I recall from my experience as a college and graduate student in Brooklyn and Princeton even during the Depression, and in the Second World War, and as a voter in the northeastern states in which I lived and voted after the War. I think this greater extremity of California's 1960's politics was an early major sign of a greater divisiveness in the American democratic process that continued and strengthened until today.

CHAPTER VII

Four Years in Manila with the Asian Development Bank

MY YEARS WITH the ADB during its early years was a great experience. It was then small in size, so that everyone knew each other and met not only professionally, but also socially so there was a real interchange. Since the Bank was then only starting its work, it had to both define what it would be doing as well as carry out that role in a more specific sense than in its general broad official guidelines. The bank staff members were from many of the Asian developing countries, who knew their own problems, as well as from Japan and other developed countries in the Asia-Pacific region, and we benefited from each others' previous experience, knowledge and ideas. The top officers of the Bank were usually open to ideas from all levels since we were genuinely working together; our relationships were beyond narrowly bureaucratic ones.

President Watanabe was related by marriage to Saburo Okita, one of Japan's major economic policy-makers and one of its leading thinkers on issues of economic development. I had met and known Mr. Okita somewhat from my earlier work in Japan and had thought very highly of his contributions to Japan's post-war recovery. In the Japanese Finance Ministry itself there is a close relationship among professional staff on policy issues – and that practice extended to the ADB under Mr. Watanabe. Toyo Gyohten, his assistant, was on leave from that Ministry. He was both open to ideas and provided easy access to the President. After his return to the Finance Ministry, he rose very rapidly and later became a major figure in the international finance field. Fusako Otahara was the President's Secretary and was both very efficient and cooperative. She left the ADB later to become a senior official of the Tokyo branch of a major American bank, an unusual post for a Japanese woman at the time. She has remained a good friend with whom I am in regular contact and whom I try to see whenever I am in Tokyo. On one of those visits to Tokyo Fusako and I also visited Mr. Watanabe and his wife at their home.

The Bank's Vice-President, C.S. Krishna Moorthy, had been a senior Indian civil servant and economic officer since Independence. He at one time had been on the staff of Prime Minister Nehru himself, then was a top Indian Finance Ministry officer before becoming India's representative on the World Bank's Board of Directors. When the ADB was established, he was appointed its Vice-President. He was a very able administrator. President Watanabe had great confidence in him, and they established a close working relationship. President Watanabe had overall supervisory responsibilities within the bank, and handled the relationships of the Bank with the governments of its member countries, especially the funding members. Vice-President Krishna Moorthy oversaw the Bank's lending and other activities in the developing countries. He knew of my work on the Indian economy although we had not met before, and he knew many of the leading Indian economists. We became good friends, remaining in touch after I left the Bank and seeing each other in Madras on my later visits to India.

My first post in the Bank was as the Deputy Director of the Projects Department, then quite small. The Director was Dr. Samuel C. Hsieh ("Sam" to his friends) from Taiwan. Sam was originally from China and had received his Ph.D. in Economics from the University of Minnesota, where he had studied with my friend, Vern Ruttan in agricultural economics. Before joining the ADB he had been Professor at the University of the Philippines College of Agriculture in Los Banos, Philippines. We had a high regard for each other's economic thinking and work both in general and in our respective fields of economic development – his in agriculture and mine in industry. We complemented each other well and cooperated smoothly. We were not competitors, spoke freely to each other exchanging opinions and advice; I recognized his superior position, working under his directorship. We remained good friends and in contact after I had left the ADB and returned to the U.S., though that contact diminished after his daughter completed her academic studies in the United States. He later became head of Taiwan's Central Bank.

A major part of my work at the Bank while in the Projects Department and later was as the Bank's loan officer for Indonesia. In the mid-1960's there had been a struggle between the government of President Sukarno, then supported by the communists, and the military, which led in effect to President Sukarno's replacement in power by General Suharto. The new government made economic development a major policy goal. President Sukarno had not been very interested in economic issues, focusing on political ones, and Indonesia had serious economic problems then. Some of the country's leading academic economists, several educated in the United States under Ford Foundation programs, became top officials in the Suharto government. They recognized the importance of dealing with Indonesia's serious short-term inflationary and long-term growth problems and sought financial aid from the ADB and other potential sources such as the U.S., Japan and the World Bank. I was asked to head the ADB's first Advisory Mission to Indonesia, which was also the Bank's first to any country. While I had no previous experience in Indonesia, the Indonesian Finance Ministry wanted an American to head the mission for the positive effect that might have on future American aid, and I was the senior American on the Bank staff; I would also carry out the industrial research work on the team. Since Indonesia was then a largely agricultural economy, there were several members of the mission who knew agricultural economics and Indonesia's rural problems. Two of these were from the Netherlands and had worked in Indonesia before its independence and in the Netherlands on Indonesian problems thereafter. After the mission completed that report, I oversaw the Bank's work there.

Our actual time spent in Indonesia on that mission was over three months. It was a most interesting visit. In Djakarta itself we were in close touch with top government economic officials, including Finance Minister Dr. Widjoyo, who had studied in the U.S. The city itself was overcrowded and not too interesting. But the country outside of Djakarta was most interesting – the regional economies had significant problems of agricultural development, trade both internally with other areas and externally with other countries, and of encouraging local entrepreneurship, and industrial development. The influence of Chinese origin inhabitants on the business side was also an important political and social issue affecting future development. The country itself was beautiful of a great scenic variety. The Borobodur Temple Complex was comparable to Angkor Wat in many ways other than size and the influence it showed of wider Hindu culture, and I enjoyed that greatly. We wrote the final version of the Mission report in Bali, before it became the major tourist center, and that was a beautiful place to work writing the report. (Not long after I was able to go to Bali with Kusum and Mark on vacation leave.) I was also struck by the complexity of Indonesian society and culture with its mix of peoples of different histories and religions on the islands composing it, and of its history prior to Dutch rule, during it and the Japanese occupation, and eventual independence. My Indonesian work with the Bank put me in touch again with Ben Higgins, who had headed up MIT's Indonesian project and with the work of Clifford Geertz, an anthropologist on that project whose books on Indonesian society were path-breaking. Heinz Arndt had established the Indonesian Center at the Australian National University and the Bank's interest in Indonesia cemented a life-long friendship that had begun in India.

An Economics Office was set up in the Bank in 1970, before the World Bank had established one, and I was appointed its first head, supervising a small professional staff. One of the first tasks of that office was to prepare a comprehensive report on Asia's economic future. That report was to be the product of a large conference with invited papers on that theme. I was in charge of preparing the agenda for that conference, and the eventual summary report, under President Watanabe's and Vice-President Krishna Moorthy's general guidance; they hosted and presided over the overall and some specific sessions of the conference. Some of the world's leading development economists were invited and came to that conference. These included Albert Hirschman, Paul Streeten, Hollis Chenery, who had only recently joined the World Bank from Harvard after Robert MacNamara had become President, Heinz Arndt, Saburo Okita, Hla Myint, then living in Burma, Sixto Roxas and Cesar Virata. I think the conference resulted in a very perceptive report. While the individual papers were never published in an overall volume, the summary report written by Hla Myint was published in a Penguin paperback volume that was widely read in Asia and elsewhere. The Economics Division also began preparing annual statistical reports on the ADB member countries' economies and these began appearing at about the time I left the Bank in mid-1971.

The Indonesian work and the Asian Economic Conference were two major specific parts of my ADB experience, but I was of course involved in one way or another with its work overall. I reviewed loan requests from member countries, related surveys and the Bank's responses to those requests. I was in contact with World Bank professional staff working in Asian countries, and with other advisory groups. In Indonesia the Ford Foundation had begun an advisory program at the government's request. This was headed by Jack Bresnan, I recall. I had known Jack when I was working with and for the Foundation in India and Nepal, and we reestablished contact in Indonesia. I renewed acquaintance there too with David Cole, working on the Harvard Economic Advisory project, who has been a close friend ever since, as is his wife, Betty Slade, an economist who also worked in Indonesia. They now live near my summer home in Cape Cod, Massachusetts, and we meet every year during the summer.

At the ADB, I also met and established long-term friendships with some other Americans whom I've been in touch with since I, and they, left the Bank and returned to the U.S. Two of these, Jeb Eddy and Peter Muncie, were speech-writers for the Bank President; Peter had been a reporter for the "Baltimore Sun" in Asia before joining the ADB and later worked for the World Bank in a major speech and report-writing capacity. Ted Mesmer, an American economist who came to the ADB from a Latin American economic background became a good friend and we have remained in touch since we left Manila.

My memory for names of old friends whom I have not seen for many years has become much worse, and I've forgotten those of others I worked with and once knew well. This is especially so for Japanese professionals who had senior positions with the Bank; Akira Tsusaka I still remember and I saw him when I visited the Bank last about ten years ago. The Filipino staff member I best remember is, Ophie Santa Ana, who worked closely with me as my assistant, and with whom I stayed in touch for some years thereafter. Liria Palafax was an economist who worked with me; we became good friends and that continued after she moved to the United States after she married an American. Vanee Lertdumrikarn was a Thai economist on the staff then. She was a very good economist and became a senior Thai government official after returning to Bangkok. We still see each other when I visit Bangkok or she comes to the United States.

We of course lived in Manila, and I have not said anything of that experience as such. The Philippines had a complex history. Before it was united, it had been an area of separate islands each with its own tribal culture and society. Many of these islands were conquered by Spanish invaders in the Fifteenth and Sixteenth centuries and combined into a country ruled by Spain and Spanish Governors. In the late Nineteenth Century there was a strong independence movement with many of its leaders imprisoned or executed by Spain. During the Spanish-American War, the Independence Movement supported the American attack on Spanish rule and seemed to have achieved its goal of independence. But Spanish rule was replaced by American rule from about 1900 to 1942, when, after Pearl Harbor, Japanese troops invaded the islands and forced out the U.S. troops. There was a Filipino underground resistance to the newly imposed Japanese rule, and in 1945 American troops recaptured the Philippines before the War ended. Some years after, the U.S. formally granted Philippine independence.

I naturally met many Filipino economists from the University of the Philippines with its strong Economic Department, and in the government. Many of them as well as the political leaders, businessmen and scholars had studied at American universities and worked with American business firms or scholarly institutions, and English was widely known. By the 1960's Spanish had been largely replaced by English as the major upper-class language, and this made it much easier for me to make Filipino friends. I got to know well Sixto Roxas, a leading businessman and then a top government official in President Marcos' government. Another top official was Cesar Virata, from an academic economic background, who became a major economic policy maker in that government. We have remained friends since then. His wife's sister, Barbara Lewis, teaches at Northwestern and is one of Sylvia Vatuk's (my second wife) oldest Chicago friends. We are in regular contact with Barbara and her husband, and through her I hear of Cesar and may see him occasionally. Another good friend from Manila then teaching Economics at the University of the Philipines, was an American economist, Richard Hooley, married to a Filipino woman. Dick and his wife came to the University of Pittsburgh, he as Economics Professor, sometime after I had returned to academic life in the U.S. He is today one of the leading American economists working on Asian economic issues, and we are in touch professionally.

Probably my closest Filipino friend in Manila was Frank Jose, and his wife Tessie. Frank and Tessie had the best book store in the city, the Solidaridad store. They also published a leading Filipino cultural and intellectual journal, "Solidarity," which was comparable to the "Economic Weekly" in Bombay. Apart from his major direct contributing role to the country's and city's intellectual and cultural life through the magazine and store, Frank himself was, and is, one of the leading contemporary novelists in the Philippines, whose books are of world stature. I think his novels of Filipino life, past and present, are both fine literature and a great introduction to the culture and society of the entire country. They would be most valuable for any scholar, including an economist, wanting to understand the Philippines, apart from the sheer enjoyment of reading them.

Kusum, Mark and I enjoyed our time in Manila. We had good friends in the families of Bank co-workers, and through our Filipino acquaintances. In Manila we enjoyed the music and dance and plays, and there were several beautiful older Spanish churches. We were able to travel to some of the lovely rural areas in northern Luzon, and by boat to Mindanao and other southern island areas. Mark enjoyed the American grammar school he went to; Kusum found the servants we had very good, and they gave her time to enjoy life outside the house. One of the external pleasures of working for the Bank were the annual conferences, often in other member countries. We visited Japan again, and, for the first time, Singapore and its neighbor Malaysia, Sydney in Australia and Vancouver in Canada for others. We enjoyed these and I still remember them.

In a broader social sense, related to my institutionalist approach to Economics, I gained an idea of Philippine society and how it worked. This was not from any direct Bank related lending and research duties since I was neither doing research about the economy nor involved in any of the Bank's loans to the government. It was apparently a quite stratified society. There was a prosperous upper and middle class of large landowning families, business groups and professional individuals and government officials and their families, many with homes in Manila and larger cities. But there were large numbers of very poor families, many working as farm laborers for the large landowners, others living in the slums of Manila and other cities and barely subsisting on casual jobs. The contrasts between the palatial homes and lovely areas in which the upper classes lived, and the city slums and poor villages where far more low income people lived were stark. Community and family relationships were major factors in national and local decision-making in both political and economic decision-making. Again, as in India, the different communal characteristics of the different parts of the country were very important in its politics. I was also struck by two other characteristics of the business people we met or dealt with. One of these characteristics, the important role of Filipinos of Chinese origin in business, was not surprising, since I also saw that in Thailand and Indonesia. There was little obvious prejudice against these businessmen and their families, and I thought that very good. The second characteristic was more surprising and unusual: that was the important role of women in businesses of all sizes, and not just as clerks, but as proprietors, managers and financial officers. I asked about that and was told that business was less prestigious for men than being in politics or in government positions at the national and local level. The very large-scale enterprises might be run by men, many educated at top American business schools, but small and medium size shops and stores were often run by women. We noticed this in many stores where we shopped, and we were told the husbands had other more prestigious jobs. This business role of women was unusual compared to that in other Asian countries I had worked in, and I considered this a positive side of the Filipino social system. Wives too seemed to handle family finances in most families I knew for the same reason. Since 1970 too women have become Presidents of the country, playing major political roles, though they became so as widows of their husbands, earlier Presidents. This has not happened yet in the United States. Before I left Manila, President Marcos had established his dictatorship, and I thought that was unfortunate; his wife played a major role in his government.

After these four years with the ADB, I thought it would be good for the family to return to the United States. I also wanted to get an academic position where I could do my own independent writing and research. My family reason was that Mark would finish grammar school shortly. I thought that because he would be living in and making a career in the U.S., he should go to college there, and attending high school in the U.S. would be important preparation for college there. It was also important that he realize that the style of our life in Manila, with servants and other luxuries we could afford because my income was high by Filipino standards, was not the American life style and would not be good preparation for his college and future life in the U.S.

I wanted to write another book. I had now worked in a range of Asian developing countries over the past twenty years. I wanted to look at the functioning of the patron-client systems, that so often characterized their traditional social sectors, in their wider policy-influencing national context. I would not be able to do that while working with the ADB, nor did I want to do that for an American policy-related center. I wanted this to be an objective picture of political-economic decision making in developing countries. I would base this on my previous work in India, Thailand, Indonesia and the Philippines in all of which I thought I had an understanding of their economic policy decision-making processes. Although I had a decade before I would have to retire from the ADB, I decided to apply to the Ford Foundation for a year's grant to write this book. I received the Ford Foundation grant. I knew "Rocky" Staples and Peter Geithner of the Ford Foundation from my previous Ford work in India. They both knew my capabilities and felt my project was a good one. During that grant year, I would work in New York, where I would have a formal connection with a New York University International Research Center. This had been arranged through Arnold Sametz, then a Professor at the NYU Business School. That would also be a good location for gathering supporting data I might need other than from my own experience and records. During that year in New York, I also planned to contact various American universities to find an academic position in the United States after I completed the year's work.

Kusum decided she would not come to New York for that year. The transition from Manila to New York city to a third place would be too difficult – she had endured many changes – and she and Mark would spend that transition year in Bombay. They would be able to live there with her sister, who had a lovely large apartment, and they would rejoin me in my new unknown location after that year.

The three of us sailed on the American President Liner, "President Cleveland," from Manila to California via Hawaii. It was a lovely trip, and I'm glad we made it. We were lucky too since I remember being told by one of the crew that this would probably be one of the last such regular passenger trips by the President Line vessels. He was right, and I regret the decision to end such voyages. For me, those long ocean trips, which I had earlier taken across the Atlantic and from India to Europe, were a wonderful vacation, an ideal way of getting away from the world, and I miss them. We flew from California to New York, from where we spent a few days together in Bridgeport with my family there. This was the first time together for some years, and there had been a great change. My uncle in Bridgeport and my step-father in Brooklyn had died during the previous few years. My mother had then sold the store and moved from Brooklyn to Bridgeport, where she lived with her sister in my aunt's home there. Helen and Sam's home was next door, which was very good since they could care for them if necessary.

Kusum and Mark flew to India, and I moved to New York soon after our visit in Bridgeport.

CHAPTER VIII

A Year of Writing and Finding an Academic Post

M Y COUSIN WALTER and his wife, Charlotte, then lived in New York. Walter was a Law Professor at Columbia Law School after having been a top legal officer in the Securities and Exchange Commission in Washington during the Kennedy-Johnson administrations. They lived on the Upper West Side of Manhattan not far from Columbia. Charlotte found a pleasant apartment for me in the Washington Square district of the city. It was within easy walking distance of my NYU office and of Arnold and Agnes Sametz's apartment. Transportation to the Ford Foundation near Grand Central was also simple, and to Walter and Charlotte's place.

The writing on my book went smoothly. I knew my theme and had the material, based on my past experience and work in the four countries, which were the focus of the volume. During that year, I met Ford staff working on Asia, and interested NYU faculty, to exchange ideas. I also gave several talks on the work at the NYU Center which hosted me. When I completed a chapter on a country, I would send that to an English language journal in that country if I knew the editor. A draft chapter on India was sent to Sachin Chaudhuri in Bombay and one on the Philippines to Frank Jose in Manila. When my research grant ended in mid-1972, the manuscript had been largely finished. This eventually became the book *Peasant Society and Economic Change*, that was published in 1974.

Apart from my work, I was very glad to be able to be near my mother and aunt, now living together in Bridgeport, and to my cousins living in and near New York. I met Walter and Charlotte at their place. Their three sons – Robert, Dan and John – were also living in or near New York, and I saw them often at Walter's or in the city. Helen and Sam lived in Bridgeport, Paul and Gladys in Danbury, and Gertrude, now a widow, not far from Danbury, all within easy reach of New York. All had children, some already started on their own careers and others in schools and colleges at various levels. Helen and Sam's oldest son, Andy, was married and was a lawyer in Bridgeport. Their youngest son, Richard, was then going to Columbia Law School in New York, and I saw him often in the city. Judy, Helen and Sam's oldest daughter, had married Al Zabin, a fellow student at Brandeis. Now he was a lawyer in Boston and Judy was doing counseling in that area. I had gotten to know them both well when I was living in Boston and working with the MIT Center. At that time too I had met Al's parents. His father had died since then. His mother, Juliet, now had an apartment on the Upper West Side of New York. We became good friends – she became like an older sister to me. I very much enjoyed going with her to art shows, concerts and plays in the city. Juliet had taken up textile artistry as a hobby, and she made some lovely decorative work. Her works often integrated woven cloth and pieces of nature such as leaves and shells, and I liked them very much. Al's sister, Dorothy, was also living near New York, and I saw her and her family at times. My step-sister Eva and her husband, Harry, who ran a large stationary store in Manhattan, were living in Brooklyn, and we met quite often, sometimes with their son, Arthur, who had finished college and started what would be a successful business career.

Apart from my writing and family relationships, New York was a great city to live in, and Washington Square, almost part of Greenwich

Village, was especially so. The theatres and music were great with a wide variety of both, and NYU offered a wide range of intellectual and cultural activities. During that year, I discovered my favorite art museum in the city – the J.P. Morgan Library, not far from Washington Square. It was not too large nor overcrowded, and had a great collection. Unlike the very large museums such as the Metropolitan or the National Gallery in Washington, I could see a show and absorb what I saw without being exhausted physically from moving through large spaces or limited by what I could see by the large crowds. I have always gone to the Morgan whenever I returned to New York after that year, although regrettably it has been closed for some time in recent years. (I feel similarly about the Phillips Gallery in Washington, D.C., and go there whenever I am in that city.)

New York has one of the widest varieties of dining places of any American city. When I worked for the U.N. at its downtown headquarters, there had been very few Indian restaurants near there. That had changed greatly. When I told my nephew Dan recently that I was writing about living in New York then, he told me that he still remembered, more than thirty years later, a question I had asked him jokingly: "Do you know a good Mongolian restaurant?" I forget his answer, but that I could ask it even as a joke shows the wide food choices that were possible. I was in regular correspondence with Kusum and Mark in Bombay. They were both well. Mark was in an English language school and Kusum and he were enjoying her family, the city she knew well and old friends of ours from when we had lived there in the late 1950's.

I was also in touch with economists and other social scientist friends living in or near New York. I knew many from my variety of non-academic jobs in or about Asia in the organizations I had worked in. My friends were at NYU, Columbia, Yale, Harvard, Pennsylvania and MIT, and I had a Princeton Ph.D. There were good friends too at universities in other parts of the country, and in international agencies such as the World Bank. With such a number of academic friends, and my own publication record – three books and numerous articles in many journals in numerous countries – I didn't think there would be any difficulty in getting a senior academic post at a major American university. While I had been out of the academic job market after I left Bard, I remembered that there had been a large demand for college faculty with the much larger enrollment after the Second World War and the Korean War. This resulted from the G.I. Bill of Rights scholarships, from which I had benefited in 1945-1946, and from postwar prosperity. When I looked for my first university job in 1946, Frank Graham had warned that I might have trouble getting one because I was Jewish. I had heard of Paul Samuelson's not being offered a Harvard position for that reason though he was already very distinguished. But from what I had observed that was no longer the case – there were many Jewish economists in the top Ivy League Schools, as well as at MIT where Samuelson and Bob Solow were in the Economics Department. I also thought my living experience in India and wider Asia and working for the U.S. government, the Ford Foundation, and the Asian Development and World Banks would be a plus for my job search, given the growing American interest in international problems and Asia.

I was overoptimistic. While I received a very nice offer from the World Bank and I felt good to get it, this was not my own top priority. I was of course glad to have that as a "fall-back" if I needed one. From universities I received only two offers: one was from the Economics Department and East-West Center of the University of Hawaii in Honolulu, based on my ADB experience. The other was from the University of Illinois at Chicago (the UIC) to become Head of the Economics Department there. I accepted that offer then, and looking back I am very glad I did.

I was surprised then that I had not received other offers and from then higher status universities. From what I have seen of academia since I rejoined it, I think I know some of the reasons. Being Jewish was not one of them. The main reasons were that I was no longer in the main stream of contemporary Economics. I was not and am not a theoretical and mathematical economist. I am essentially an institutional economist using statistics if I need them. I write in English that both an economist and intelligent layman can read, partly reflecting my non-academic policy-oriented experiences of twenty years. That experience too was overseas in developing countries with different economies, social structures and economic histories than the United States and Western Europe. When I had studied Economics and practiced it, these were not disadvantages. But since the 1950's Economics had become more of a "science"; theory and mathematical techniques had become dominant in this country. Thorstein Veblen is considered more of a sociologist than an economist by today's economists, and Institutional Economics is not mainstream. Public policy analysis, rather than the primary focus of the subject, is now secondary. Prediction has become more important, as part of business analysis. Academic economic literature is in large part mathematical, written for other economists rather than a wider audience. The great economists I had read, from Adam Smith to John Maynard Keynes who sought to influence public thinking and economic policies and wrote in English, with Math in appendices, are today often unread; the History of Economic Thought is no longer a major area of interest. To work in other societies with histories, cultures and social structures different from those of the West calls for acquiring a knowledge of those societies and the functioning of their economies. That takes time and that time not spent on publishing articles in leading western economic journals makes it difficult to get tenure in American Economics Departments. Interest too in developing countries has declined over time in academia, and Development Economics was becoming a marginal field during the early 1970's when I was making my move. I did not realize this when I decided I wanted to return to academia, and I think those factors contributed to my offers being fewer than what I had expected.

UIC was looking for an external head of its Economics Department for 1972 because of internal splits within the department. Irving Heckman, then the Dean of the College of Business Administration (CBA), in which the Economics Department was and is, thought it desirable to find an outsider as new head, to resolve those intra-department disagreements. He chose Professor Robert Ferber to head the Search Committee for that new Head. Bob Ferber was not from the UIC faculty, but from the University of Illinois at Urbana Economics Department Faculty. Professor Frances Flanagan represented the UIC Department on that committee. Both Bob and Fran were very interested in their own research on policy-related economic issues. It turned out that Adolf Sturmthal was then a colleague of Bob's at Urbana. Adolf had left Bard some years earlier to become Labor Economics Professor at Urbana and then directed a research center on labor economic issues. Adolf of course knew me well from Bard and we had remained good friends. I had written him of my wish to return to academic life. He had then told me of the UIC opening and suggested I apply. I am sure Bob's positive response to my application must have been influenced by recommendation from Adolf, though he never told me of it. I did and later attended the 1971 American Economic Association meeting where I was interviewed by Bob and Fran.

Following that preliminary interview, I was invited to meet Dean Heckman and the Economics Department at UIC in Chicago in early 1972. Dean Heckman would decide whether or not to make an offer after that visit. I went to Chicago, gave a talk to the Department and met the Dean. I spoke about my work as an economist at a department seminar and met some of the faculty; I spoke to the Dean about the duties of Department Head and my own past administrative experience. In the department itself, I only knew personally Eliezer Ayal, who had recently joined it, from my time at RAND and his work in Thailand. I was very glad he was on the faculty because he was a development economist, and I thought highly of his work in Thailand. I also knew well the work of William Grampp, a major historian of economic thought and a former student of Frank Knight's at Chicago. I had always regarded Knight as one of America's leading economists and Bill had edited his works. I had found Bill's own work very readable and interesting. While at Chicago, I also met socially Fran Flanagan, living near the University of Chicago where her then husband worked. I was staying at the University of Chicago Quadrangle Club, and Fran invited me for a very pleasant dinner at her home near there. Bert Hoselitz, a long-time friend from his work on India, on the University of Chicago Economics Faculty and Editor of the journal "Economic Development and Cultural Change," also lived nearby, and I saw him on that visit. The University of Chicago had three other development economists who had worked in India, Pakistan and China, whom I had met at one time or another and whose work I knew well: Harry Johnson, Ted Schultz and Gale Johnson.

Dean Heckman did make an offer to me, and I decided to accept it for several reasons. Chicago was much closer to my family on the east coast than Honolulu. I liked the economists whom I had met at UIC and the closeness of University of Chicago economists whose work I already knew, and one of whom, Bert, was a good friend. UIC was also appealing to me because it reminded me of my own Brooklyn College education. I felt by working in an urban, low-tuition state university I could help lower-income families in Chicago, many black, by educating their children, as Brooklyn College had helped low-income Jewish students like myself. Another attraction of Chicago as a place in which to live was that Robie and Ann Macauley were working and living there. Robie and I had roomed together at BARD. He was now Fiction Editor at "Playboy Magazine" and also was a Guest Professor in the UIC English Department. They were good friends, and I was glad to be near them. While I was not attracted by the administrative duties of Department Head, I thought I could learn these within two or three years, given my past administrative experience at ADB, and also do the required teaching and then concentrate on my research which was my main reason for returning to academia. Adolf Sturmthal had also told me he thought that with its location in Chicago, a major city and intellectual center, the UIC campus would, over 10-15 years, become as good as the Urbana campus of the University of Illinois because it would attract top quality faculty. That of course added to its appeal.

Once I made the decision, I contacted Kusum and Mark, asking them to come to New York in about June. She and Mark would see my family again, and we would then go to Chicago. We would find a house and the high school where Mark would begin in September. After we identified a house, I would contact the ADB in Manila, which had kept our furniture and other heavy items in storage, to ship the stuff to our new address.

CHAPTER IX

Heading a Department and Starting a New Life in Chicago

W HEN WE ARRIVED in Chicago that summer, our first task was to find a place to live and to settle in. We found a house in Wilmette, a pleasant northern suburb which we were told had a very good high school. It was within an hour's drive from the UIC campus, which was also reachable by the suburban train system. The house we bought was in Wilmette's western area near the main highway from the city. We also bought a car soon after we arrived. Once we got the house we contacted the ADB asking it to ship the stuff in storage to Chicago as soon as possible, and we bought furniture we would need to settle in before that came. I learned later that not many Jewish families could have bought houses in that suburb some years earlier, but this was not the case in the recently developed area where our house was. Mark began at New Trier West High School in Wilmette when the term started in September. There were also families from India living in Wilmette, and we met some of these socially soon after we arrived.

I began my work at UIC as soon as we arrived. I had to learn how the Economics Department functioned, my relationship with the Dean's office and my actual job as Head. I was told that as Department Head I had the decision-making responsibility under the Dean. There was a Faculty Advisory Committee, elected by the faculty, but its role was purely advisory to me. The courses being offered were the normal Economics courses, and faculty members could suggest additional specialized courses. My office made the teaching assignments and schedules, after meeting with the Advisory Committee, and the teachers themselves. I also had authority to make recommendations for annual pay increases, on promotions and tenure decisions and on hiring of new faculty, including the offers to prospective faculty. My recommendations would go to the Dean of CBA who would have to approve them before implementation. I discussed my recommendations with the Advisory Committee, but the Committee's approval was not required for my decision – I might or might not accept its advice.

There was an Administrative Officer in the Department whose job it was to assist me in this decision-making and do the required paperwork. Geri Kennedy was the officer when I began my work, and she held that post as long as I was Head. She did an excellent job, and we became good friends quite apart from her work. We remained friends after I quit the Headship and after she left UIC until she died in the 1990's at an early age.

I met faculty members who were in Chicago that summer before I began work officially in September. Within the Department then were about five faculty whose specialization was Finance. They asked me if I had any objection if a separate Finance Department were set up in the College. I told them I did not – I had always considered Economics and Finance as two separate fields. I informed the Dean of my opinion when the request for a separate Finance Department was made to him, and he set up that department. In addition to the Finance centered faculty I of course met the economists within the department. As mentioned, I had known Elie Ayal, then at University of California, when I had been at RAND before I went to Thailand. I knew Bill Grampp's work well and had met Fran Flanagan through her Search Committee appointment, but I knew no others beyond meeting them when I was being recruited in the Spring. I liked those I met personally, but did not know their backgrounds, past economic work or current research interests.

The University of Illinois' Chicago campus had only recently been established as a four year college, on its permanent location. After the War, with the G.I. Scholarship program underway, an undergraduate campus had been set up in Chicago at a temporary location on an uncertain status within the University of Illinois system. It was first regarded as an intermediate step toward the undergraduate and graduate degrees given at Urbana, which was then the only campus of the University offering B.A. and graduate degrees. With Chicago the largest city in the State, there was obvious need for a state campus there after the Second World War, and strong political pressure from the city's mayors to establish a permanent Chicago campus of the University. One was approved, and constructed by the mid-1960's, with its own administrative structure within the University. A College of Business Administration was established within that campus – an obvious need in one of the country's leading economic centers – and the Economics Department was in that College, as it was on the Urbana campus. My own belief, derived from my Economics education, was that the Economics Department should be in a Humanities or Liberal Arts College, but the UIC decision had been made long before I came there. That created no problem for me. Dean Heckman, who hired me, and Ralph Westfall, who succeeded him as Dean during my five years as Head, strongly supported my work.

The faculty in the Department were very able economists in their respective fields, but because UIC had only recently been established, many of them came from the University of Chicago and Northwestern University, the two leading Chicago area universities. In general they were trained in the mathematical econometric approach that dominated the discipline, although Bill Grampp and Oscar Miller, another pre-War University of Chicago graduate, were exceptions, as was Elie Ayal from Israel and with his interest in Asia. Fran Flanagan and Woods Bowman had a broad public policy approach. My predecessor as department head, Dick Kosobud, was a very able econometrician, who had been a student of Lawrence Klein; Houston Stokes and Ron Moses from

Chicago, John McDonald from Yale, and Mildred Levy from Northwestern were skilled, mathematically oriented economists. The CBA Budget gave the Economics Department funds to add one economist per year to the faculty and to replace any member who left, during the five years I was Head. I decided in my first year that I would try to find new faculty both from a broad national range of universities and with theoretical and methodological approaches to Economics other than a free competitive market approach or a highly mathematical one. I also wanted to get faculty from other countries and experience than just the United States. I contacted numerous economist friends I had met in my work outside of the university, as well as those from universities I had been associated with in some way or other. I also used the usual economist market channels such as the American Economic Association. During my five years, I hired Gilbert Bassett from Michigan, Mo Yin Tam from Hong Kong and SUNY Stony Brook, where she had studied with Egon Neuberger, my friend from MIT,. Joseph Persky from Harvard then teaching at a southern university, Antonio Camacho from Spain and Minnesota, Will White from Harvard, Jose Alberro from Mexico and Chicago and Ali Akarca from Turkey and Northwestern. They also had different fields of interest. Those fields included urban development, macro-economics, health economics and economic development. Some approached the subject from radical and historical approaches, as well as from a competitive market approach with a mathematical technique.

In addition to my appointments I made a strong effort to expand interchange of ideas among the faculty. I was struck by how little there was of such exchange compared to what I had observed at Brooklyn and Princeton when I was a student, or at the MIT Center or RAND. I encouraged intra-department seminars on work in progress and for social exchange. Kusum and I began having regular get-togethers at our home so that we would get to know each other as friends and associates, and certainly not as competitors. As I lived longer in the Chicago area, I felt the lack of such social exchange was in part a result of the distances we lived from each other. When I was a student at Brooklyn the faculty had lived in the city and at Princeton near its campus. At Bard when I first taught, we all lived near each other. In Chicago, however, many of us lived in suburban areas distant from the campus, which was in the center of the city, and we were far from each other. This was partly because the public schools for our children were much better in the suburbs than in Chicago itself. We invited department faculty and staff families to our place so that we would meet socially and as friends.

As mentioned, I was responsible for recommending annual faculty pay increases, promotions in rank and grants of tenure to the current faculty. It took a great deal of effort to evaluate faculty research and teaching. For this evaluation the assistance of my Advisory Committee was essential, especially since I was not mathematical. I needed advice on the quality of articles relying on econometric methods. The number of articles published or accepted in a year had become the major criterion of research unlike in my own earlier academic generation when an article's contribution to the field or its public policy relevance, or a book in progress, were given greater consideration. I evaluated teaching by actually visiting classes being taught, and by written student evaluations and talks with the students of a teacher. Another consideration was the faculty member's contribution to the Department itself and the wider campus by membership on committees on levels ranging from within the department, to the college to the entire campus.

I still remember the relatively low salary of Bill Grampp at the time. He was the faculty member whose work I had known for the longest time before I came. I regarded his work on the history of economic thought and his collection of Frank Knight's articles as major contributions to Economics. But because he was one of UIC's earliest faculty members his starting UIC salary had been of the late 1940's, with only low annual percentage increases within the state budget thereafter. Since he liked Chicago, he didn't seek bargaining increases by getting offers from non-Chicago universities, nor was he interested in a higher paying administrative position at UIC. His salary was low for someone of his stature, in comparison with new faculty hired at current market salaries. When I learned that I could recommend a "higher than average" pay increase to adjust for a situation such as his, I did that in his case, though he did not ask for it.

In 1972 the Economics Department offered an M.A. degree, but not a Ph.D. Over the next several years the UIC Graduate College was developing a Ph.D. program in Public Policy Analysis which included Liberal Arts departments such as Political Science. I strongly recommended to the Dean of the Graduate College to include the Economics Department in the Ph.D. program and urged Dean Heckman to support that recommendation, which he did. The Graduate College Dean accepted this. Economics was included and as a result the Economics Department was able to offer a Ph.D. degree for the first time, once the program was approved by the responsible highest level university decision makers, while I was still department head.

I brought two other issues to the attention of the department faculty before I left as Head. The first was whether the department should change from the "benevolent despotism" of a Headship to the possible greater democracy of a Chairmanship. I raised this with the faculty, and they voted to appoint a committee to report on the functioning of Chairmanships in those campus departments that had Chairs rather than Heads and to make a recommendation. The committee did interview the Chairs and faculty in those departments, and recommended against such a move. Decision-making in Chair-led departments was apparently more time consuming and difficult than under Heads, which is probably correct. There might also have been some committee members who saw themselves as possible Heads, and saw greater difficulty if they became Chairs instead.

The second issue was whether Economics should move to the College of Liberal Arts. I had long believed that Economics was separate from Business Administration. The faculty voted against that move I think in large part because salaries in CBA were higher than in Liberal Arts. They worried they would lose by the shift, which I fully understood.

I also was teaching while I was Head. While this was then part-time, I still had to prepare those courses I taught since I had not taught for twenty years. The courses were in my fields of Economic Development and Public Policy Analysis. I enjoyed the teaching more than I expected. It still makes me very happy when one of my former students from that time remembers one of those courses and tells me how much he or she got from it.

But the Headship and associated responsibilities took all my efforts. I had anticipated it would become more routine after a few years and then I could do my own research. But the work of Head was never routine. I was working with twenty individuals who were also my colleagues, each with his or her needs and problems which I had to discuss and resolve, and I was also searching for new faculty. All of this never became routine. While I completed and published the book I wrote in 1971-1972 on my Ford grant, I did not have time to do new research. That was the reason I had returned to academic life. I therefore decided to give up the Headship after my fifth year. I felt I had fulfilled my commitment when I was hired, and I had learned much about the new academic life and UIC. I was asked if I wanted to be considered for the Deanship after Irv Heckman left that post, but I wasn't interested.

My book *Peasant Society and Economic Change* was published in 1974. I had submitted it first to the University of California Press as I was legally committed to do by my contract for my previous book that it had published. They did not accept the manuscript, and I now sent it to the University of Illinois Press. The Chicago based editor of the Press was Frank Williams. The Press accepted the manuscript and published it after a good editing job. Frank and his wife, Jean, became good friends during that whole process, and we remained friends ever since. The book received little recognition in this country, getting a few small notices in economic journals. It was, however, well received in Asia. The review in "Opinion" magazine in Bombay was by H.M. Patel, who had been one of colonial India's former major Economic policy officials in the ICS before Independence and the Finance Ministry until he retired. He later became Finance Minister. He thought highly of the India chapter especially, and of the book. It was also reviewed in a leading Southeast Asian Economic journal by the former Finance Minister of Singapore who had played a major role in that country's development. He considered it the best book written by an economist on economic policy-making in Asia until that date, a comment which made me feel very good, coming from such a knowledgeable person. I was disappointed in the absence of any American review in an economic journal when the book appeared, but later, after teaching Economics here for some time, I was not surprised. It was not mathematical, and it was inter-disciplinary, crossing fields of Anthropology and Politics with Economics.

Such books were rarely reviewed in Economic journals in this country in the 1970's, when it was published, nor unfortunately has this changed.

I was invited for conferences in Asia or as a consultant with economic organizations in Asia. In so participating, I spent brief periods with ECAFE (the Economic Commission for Asia and the Far East) in Bangkok, the ADB in Manila, and in India during summers or between terms. These were opportunities to see old friends again and to gain an impression of current events, but they were not research opportunities.

In Chicago itself I met friends working on India – the University of Chicago was one of the leading American centers of Indian studies, with some of the major economists in this country who were working on India and Pakistan. Milton Singer, Kim Marriott and other leading anthropologists were also there then, working on India. At UIC itself no one in Economics other than myself worked on India, but Elie Ayal was a leading economist on Thailand. Scarlett Epstein visited Kusum and me in Wilmette on a trip from England. She knew Paul Hockings, a Professor in the UIC Anthropology Department who worked in South India. On her visit to us we invited Paul to meet her at our place. I enjoyed meeting him, and we became good friends. Apart from his work on India he was interested in economic anthropology, a field which interested me. Paul in turn introduced me to his colleague in Anthropology, Sylvia Vatuk, who had done extensive research in North India. There was no other India interest on the UIC campus then. Kusum and I also enjoyed meeting both Paul and Sylvia and Sylvia's husband, Ved. He was an Indian poet and linguist from North India whom Sylvia had met in England when they were students together at the University of London. At Urbana, Harold Gould in the Political Science Department was doing important research on Indian politics. I met him through Paul and Sylvia, who already knew him, and we became good friends, exchanging ideas on the Indian political economy.

Apart from people working on India or Economics I met many faculty in other fields during those first years at UIC. They were met as neighbors in or near Wilmette. One occasion was through a faculty wives club that had been formed and which met fairly often. Among those neighbors were Bernie Kogan and Roger Little, both in the Social Sciences. The longest friend and colleague among my then neighbors was Manuel Blanco Gonzalez in the Spanish Department and his wife, Elfriede. He was a linguist, author and poet, and Elfriede had come to the United States as a student from Germany after the war. Manuel died very recently and somewhat unexpectedly – a real personal loss. The other means of meeting non-economists was by being on committees with them, and it was by such work I met Nancy Cirillo in the English Department, a good friend since. One of my best friends was Irving Thalberg in the Philosophy Department. He was the son of Norma Shearer, the great movie star. We became good friends after serving on a committee because we both liked movies, and we would go together to films playing in Chicago. I of course became good friends over time with the economists I had hired for the Department and with those already there, and their wives or husbands. Mo Yin Tam, Joe Persky, Tony Camacho, Gib Bassett and Ali Akarca are still in the Department or College and living in or near Chicago. Will White left for Yale and Cornell with his wife, but I try to stay in touch. Jose Alberro returned to Mexico and I lost contact. Among the faculty when I joined Ron Moses and his wife, Jackie, became very close friends. Jackie is one of Chicago's major painters, whose work I very much like and have. Ron was a very insightful economist, who died of cancer quite recently at an early age – and that was a real personal loss. Millie Levy, now Millie Marnin, has remained a close friend, after leaving Economics and UIC, becoming first a lawyer and then an artist.

Of the Department members of my generation who were there when I came, Bill Grampp has remained a good friend. He was the one whose work I then found most interesting, and his later work on the economics of art has also been of great pleasure. History of thought and art have always been major interests of mine, and Bill is always readable, though I may not always agree. Oscar Miller was my other contemporary. He was a great teacher and was Dean of Students when I came to UIC. Elie Ayal's work in my own field I knew well and regarded highly, and I strongly urged his promotion, but that did not happen until after my term as Head. I have largely lost touch with Oscar and Elie, who don't live near where I do.

As a department head in the CBA, I met the other heads regularly. We served as an advisory group to the Dean and got to know each other. One of those, Bob Weigand, who headed the Marketing Department for many years, became my closest friend in the College outside the Department. He has a major research interest in Japan, doing work on Japanese business, and has spent much time there. That country has been one of my interests since 1950, having worked on its economy, lived there, and worked with Japanese colleagues. Bob enjoys classical music very much, we enjoy Chicago Symphony matinee programs together, and he too likes art. We see each other often in Chicago, though no longer as Department Heads, but as good friends.

After Irv Heckman left the Deanship, we didn't see each other often. Since he lived in a rather distant suburb, we lost touch socially as well. He died recently. However, I have stayed in touch with his successor, Ralph Westfall, and his wife Charlotte, living in Evanston. We were friends in the CBA and have continued to see each other since we retired. They had once lived in India for a year on a visiting academic appointment so that country is a joint interest, and we have other common interests as well.

In the next chapter I will write about my work after the five years I was Head. It will focus on my research, but I was also doing teaching and department committee work. I met my older colleagues and those newly hired after my headship, as associates in the department, and made other friends from other departments on campus. But so far in this chapter I have said nothing of my life with Kusum and Mark and other family during those first years in Chicago. That was a very eventful period of my life.

My mother and aunt were living together in their home in Bridgeport when we moved to Chicago in 1972. Both were in their eighties then, but in good health, with Helen and Sam living next to them. Helen remembers that my mother would walk every morning to the newspaper stand several blocks from the house to get the New York Times, and she would be greeted by neighbors on the way. My aunt too was very active around the house and garden. My mother had a minor stroke about a year after coming to Bridgeport, but had recovered quickly. I visited in Bridgeport several times during those first years by myself and at times with Kusum and Mark. They would come with me during Mark's summer vacations and possibly on mid-term holidays. My mother and aunt were very glad to see us, and we enjoyed the visits with them and other family.

But in the summer of 1974 my mother had a major stroke that left her in a coma and unable to move or speak. She went to the hospital and then to a nursing home, where she was fed by a tube and was on constant sedation. She saw little and recognized no one as far as we could tell. Helen and Sam were able to take care of her in that condition. I came as often as I was able to, but could do little. That summer Kusum and Mark had gone to India to be with Kusum's family; their return would be of no help. A doctor came to see my mother regularly, but he could do little. I asked him whether it might not be preferable if she were allowed to die since she was not alive in any real sense. He said that was illegal, apart from any other issue. So she continued in a coma until she eventually died.

Meanwhile my aunt was having her own health problems. Her doctor recommended she have an overall medical exam including comprehensive blood tests at the nearby hospital. She went there for those tests. In one of those tests of arteries a mistake was made. Instead of inserting the needle into the proper place, it was inserted into her intestinal system, resulting in a flow of body waste into her blood stream. That was fatal, and she died before my mother. My mother of course was never aware of her sister's passing away. Her death, and soon after my mother's, was the most traumatic emotional experience I think I've had. My mother and aunt had brought me from Russia, raised me as a boy and supported me in school and their almost simultaneous deaths was a great blow. I went to their funerals and burials in Bridgeport, with my cousins and their families. Helen and Sam's support was vital, especially since Kusum could not be there. On my mother's burial stone I had engraved a line from one of the poems written by her friend, Marianne Moore, who had died a few years before her.

During those five years, Mark was growing up. He graduated from High School, where he did well academically, and was on the wrestling team – very unusual for anyone in my family – and some of his classmates became good friends. He then began college at Lawrence College in Wisconsin, a small, very good college several hundred miles north of Chicago. He was doing well and adjusting nicely to living in the United States from what I could tell. Our intimate relations were not close. As I mentioned earlier, my own relationships with my parents had not been close. I may have repeated my experience with Mark. I think his relationship with his mother was closer. He and Kusum certainly spent more time together in the many places we had lived before Wilmette, and he and she had been together for a year in India when I had been in New York before Chicago.

I separated from Kusum at the end of those five years. When I had come back from India in 1956 after our marriage, I remember seeing the counselor in Washington whom I had consulted about my relationship with Garland Draper. I saw him in 1956 as a friend while I was in Washington from Cambridge for some other reason, to tell him that I had married a lovely Indian woman. He had congratulated me, but had also warned me that there were risks in such a marriage with our very different cultural backgrounds.

Kusum was beautiful and most supportive of my decisions where I worked and where we would live. She handled much of the moving and resettling. Those moves were not easy for her and could not have been satisfying. She was very happy to have Mark, and took care of him as he was growing, while I worked and moved about. But we did not have very much in common in our intellectual and cultural interests. When Scarlett visited us in Chicago, she remarked before she left that Kusum had not talked to her and seemed to dislike her and my exchanges with her on our work. Kusum had little interest in western literature, art or music, all of which I like – we went to movies together and that was it. In India and other countries where we lived this had not raised any problem. We both enjoyed Indian culture and its music, dance and art, and in other Asian countries, and she enjoyed social exchanges with wives in those countries. But in Chicago the women we knew were academic professionals, and she had little in common with them.

As I mentioned, one of the only two other UIC faculty working then on India was Sylvia Vatuk in Anthropology, and Kusum and I had become friends with her and her husband. They divorced in 1976. I met Sylvia quite often professionally at conferences and when we overlapped briefly in India. We became good friends and our friendship developed into a closer relationship. She had similar intellectual and cultural interests to those I had, and our political and social points of view were similar. In about 1977 I decided to separate from Kusum and I got my own apartment in Evanston, while she stayed in the Wilmette house. I did not get a divorce, and Mark lived with her when he came from college.

During that year, my relations with Sylvia became closer, and after that year we decided to live together. I moved to her house in Evanston, where she lived with her four children whom she was raising. Her former husband had returned to India. During that year, I also met her parents, who lived in Rhode Island, and we bought a small summer place together in Bristol, Rhode Island. I decided to divorce Kusum. In the divorce settlement I agreed to give her all our property and share half of whatever salary I earned thereafter as alimony. The judge who handled our divorce thought that was very fair; he added that the fifty percent share of my salary after the divorce as alimony should not continue from my non-salary retirement income. Since we had been married for over twenty years, she would receive Social Security income also, plus any alimony I might voluntarily give her after I retired – which I do give. We have remained in touch, and she now lives in Florida.

Sylvia and I were married in 1979. I thought this might be performed by a Jewish reform rabbi since I considered myself Jewish in an ethnic but not religious sense. Sylvia had no objection, but the rabbi I asked would not do that unless Sylvia converted to Judaism. She had no such intention, and neither of us were religious. We were married by a Unitarian minister at our home in Evanston in a civil ceremony during Thanksgiving weekend. We celebrated our 25th anniversary in 2004. Sylvia's children and parents were there and various Chicago friends. After the wedding, Frank and Jean Williams held a lovely reception for us at their home in Evanston, Mark came for the reception, and we were very glad he did.

CHAPTER X

Research and Teaching at UIC

N OW THAT I was no longer Head I could do the research of my own choice, which was why I had returned to university life. One of my main interests had always been public policy making in economically related fields – much of my career had been devoted to this. A Chicago issue that interested me very much from the time I first came to UIC was the decision to locate the UIC campus where it was built. That decision had aroused much controversy that had extended over the terms of three mayors before it was finally made by Mayor Daley. It would have economic aspects, and I thought I would like to do a major study of that decision, which would also introduce me to Chicago's history and functioning, of which I knew little. I applied to the University of Illinois for a research grant and leave for the year after I left the headship to do that project. I got the leave and the grant for 1977-1978. The University was very interested in the project which centered on its own history, and was very supportive.

It was a productive year, and I did the research I needed for the book on that location decision. I interviewed University officials, including the Presidents involved in that decision-making and then Chicago faculty, on the early history of the campus, and saw all the records the University had. I did likewise with the city and state officials who were still accessible to get their pictures of how the decisions were made and what factors affected them. Economic choices were not important for those decisions. The city's economic availabilities set the framework for the decision, and some of the economic hopes and consequences from it influenced its reception. The location was in the city's old Italian neighborhood, part of which had become an urban city-controlled development area. There was strong opposition to the campus among many of the Italian residents, though the alderman and some businessmen favored it. I interviewed Florence Scala, who led the local opposition to the decision, and she lent me her files for that battle – and we became lifelong friends; I also interviewed the district alderman and various real estate and other businessmen for their views of what happened then. I think I learned a good deal about Chicago by that research – its history, its decision-making and its neighborhood characteristics – that I would never have learned otherwise and which transcended economics in a narrow sense.

An additional pleasure I gained from that research was from a trip to Asheville, North Carolina. I made that trip to interview one of Chicago's former top city officials who had been involved in the decision and had retired to Asheville. I had told Robie and Ann that I was going there, and they told me that Garland, Ann's sister with whom I had a long relationship before we separated, was working and living there. I had not seen her for about twenty years. We met once or twice in Asheville, and I was very glad to see her once more. While we wrote a few times to each other thereafter, we never met again, and some years later Robie told me that she had died.

The Chicago Historical Society supported that project as part of its interest in the history of Chicago's neighborhoods. It had excellent photographs of the Italian neighborhood, and records of its history. I was given access to these records, they published a summary of my work in the Society's journal, reprinted later in a collection of that journal's articles, and allowed me to use some of their photos for my book on the research. That book, *Decision-Making Chicago Style*, was published in 1979 by the University of Illinois Press with the strong support of Frank Williams, its Chicago editor and a close friend.

The book was well received in Chicago and reviewed in Chicago papers, and read quite widely in the UIC campus community and by interested city people, but it had little wider reception. It went out of print and was not republished, probably due to its low sales. I learned later that all the copies the UIC Library had on its shelves had disappeared. A copy was not available about twenty years later when Robert Remini and various colleagues in the UIC History Department were working on a history of UIC. I xeroxed a copy of my own copy for them. I recently met Leon Despres, who had been the independent alderman from the Hyde Park district of the city when that UIC location decision was being made. I asked him if he had ever seen the book; he had not, and I thought he might be interested. I was wondering, years after the decision, whether he thought it was a good picture of the decision-making process on that issue. I was very glad when he told me that he liked the book and thought it did give a good picture of what happened. I don't think there were any reviews of the book in any of the economic journals or any recognition of it in the profession. It was far out of the mainstream.

One great long-term benefit from it was my friendship with my research assistant, Ahmad Seifi. Ahmad was an Economics graduate student at UIC and had been one of my students in my Economic Development class. He was from Iran and a good economist and statistician. He did much of the statistical work for that research which was most helpful. We became good friends then and remained close friends after he got his Ph.D. and returned to Iran. We have remained good friends and try to see each other with our families whenever he is in the United States. His wife, Nooshin, has become a good friend also.

While I wrote that book after only six years at UIC, I think, after thirty years of association with that campus and living in its neighborhood, that the location decision was a good one and fortunate for the city, though it had some immediate negative effects on the Italian community. Putting the campus near the center of the city made it much easier for students to come there from all parts of the city and from various social groups, than if it had been placed in some less central area, or a suburb. At the time too there was no alternative. I was told later that if that site had not been selected and a campus not built there the University, which had waited for a long time for a choice to be made, might have used the money for some other purpose, outside of Chicago, to avoid losing it.

My next major research project was to examine the past experience of foreign economic advisors in two of the countries where they had given advice, in the hope that such a review might be useful for future advisory work in other countries. I had been an advisor myself, or associated with advisors, in different Asian countries over the previous twenty years while working with the MIT Center, the Ford Foundation, World Bank and the ADB, and I thought my historical perspective would be of interest and useful to others. I decided to look at the histories of the MIT Center project in India, funded entirely by the Ford Foundation after 1958, and Harvard's Pakistan project. I had been a research economist on the MIT project in Bombay before 1959, though not as an advisor in New Delhi, and I knew economists working with the Planning Commission. I also knew many of the Harvard economists associated with the Harvard project as friends from my time in Cambridge and India. My interest in that research which I began then was partly stimulated by the fact that both the Harvard and MIT projects were ended for political reasons by the governments of the countries being advised. In Pakistan a new government which overthrew the government the Harvard group had previously been advising, sent the advisors back to the U.S. as evidence of change. The MIT Center was caught between two sides in a disagreement within the Indian government over economic planning policy. Max Millikan had spoken to Mr. B.K. Nehru, the Indian Ambassador to the U.S., of the desirability of reducing overall economic controls and restrictions on private Indian business firms in order to stimulate growth. The Ambassador was convinced by those suggestions, based on the experiences of the advisors, and passed them to Prime Minister Nehru. This move was strongly opposed by the Planning Commission, where the MIT economists worked. One of the Commission staff revealed the fact that the MIT Indian project had been partly funded by the CIA in its earliest years. Prime Minister Nehru had been told that before the

MIT Center began its work and the top Indian government economic officers had always known it. But it was clearly politically sensitive and was never public. Its public release, though it was no longer the case, threatened political problems for the Congress Party government and the Center's advisory project was ended. Ambassador Nehru's suggestion for reducing controls, which economists in the Planning Commission opposed, was not followed up.

I wanted to explore these experiences as a guide for future work by foreign economic advisors in developing countries, as well as in other countries with different cultures and political systems than their own. They should be aware of the political and broader environment in which they work, and their advice cannot be purely economic in a technical sense if it is to be acceptable to the government being advised. I did much of my research for that project on leave from UIC in 1980-1981. I received grants for that year from the Social Science Research Council and the American Institute of Indian Studies (AIIS) to do my research in the United States in Cambridge at MIT and Harvard, at the Ford Foundation in New York, and in India, to look at records and interview economists associated with the work in Pakistan and India. I also went to Pakistan and India to meet economists and officials in both countries who had worked with the Harvard advisors in Pakistan and the MIT economists in India. I of course knew many of the Indian economists from my own work there. There were others from Pakistan whom I had met while I lived in Cambridge, or who worked for the ADB, Ford Foundation and World Bank. I was very glad to see old friends and colleagues who were very helpful and passed on their experiences. The MIT Center staff and Ford Foundation librarians were highly cooperative in making their records available. The book *Western Economists and Eastern Societies*, based on that research, was published in 1985 by the Johns Hopkins University Press, as part of a series it had just begun on economic development. It had some reviews but not many – again it crossed disciplines and was not mainstream Economics. I was glad to hear later from friends that it did have some influence on the later Harvard advisory programs in other countries. Ed Mason told me he liked the book which made me feel proud. Don Blackmer wrote his book on the history of the MIT Center in 2003 for its 50th anniversary.

He then told me my book had been very useful for him which I was glad to hear.

One of the pleasures in doing the research for that book was the several months I was in New York exploring the relevant Ford Foundation records and interviewing old friends there. I stayed then in Lore Segal's apartment on the Upper West Side conveniently located by subway to Foundation offices. Lore was a colleague of Sylvia and me at UIC, where she taught Creative Writing in the English Department. When she was in Chicago, she shared our apartment there. She was a widow with two children living in a very attractive apartment with art I very much liked. Her mother, Franzi, lived in an apartment in the same building, and I very much enjoyed meeting her then. I saw Franzi recently, close to her 100th birthday, at the home she is in now, and she remembered me. Being in New York was, as always, pleasant in other respects also – its museums, plays and concerts are great. But I also realized I preferred Chicago which has the same variety of pleasures more conveniently available for us where we live in that city.

A great pleasure was to be with my cousin Walter again, and his wife, Nan. Charlotte, his first wife and mother of his three sons, who had been a close and great friend of mine, had died an early death in the 1970's. Several years after her death, Walt had met Nan, an author living in the area, and they married. I had met Nan for the first time before their marriage and liked her very much. I was very happy for both of them when I heard of their marriage. They had a very pleasant apartment near Central Park in the West Sixties, and I enjoyed frequent visits there, where I met Walt's sons when they were in town. I went to Bridgeport to see Helen and Sam, and to Danbury to see Paul and Gladys, and Gert, living near there. If they came to New York, as they did several times while I was there, we'd meet then.

Arnold and Agnes Sametz were living near NYU where they had lived in 1972, and I saw them of course. Al and Ginny Karchere lived near New York. Al headed IBM's Economics office at its headquarters outside the city, and I visited there.

After that year's research and writing, I went back to teaching for several years. My next major research was in India in 1983-1984. I had not been back to India for extended research on its industrial development since the early 1960's. While I had kept up with what was happening economically and on my visits had talked to economists and others I knew about industrial change there, I had done no intensive research. I decided I wanted to do that. I applied for leave from UIC and for a research grant for the research from the AIIS and received the grant and leave. Sylvia also wanted to do anthropological research there in 1983-1984. Her research would center on Muslim women in India and she planned to do this in Hyderabad. Hyderabad is a city with a large Muslim population. Before it became a state in independent India, it was the capital of a princely state ruled by a Muslim prince. It was now the capital of one of South India's leading states, Andhra Pradesh, with one of India's leading universities and a state government interested in the state's economic development. In my research I planned to examine both India's overall industrial development since my earlier research in the 1950's, and the problems of growth in south India in particular.

The year was a good one. Hyderabad was a pleasant place to live, and our apartment was near where the University's Economics and Anthropology Departments then were in the city itself. Sylvia knew Urdu, the language widely used in the city and state, which was a big help socially, and her work went well. I had close, friendly relations with the economists in the Economics Department and others in the area. The Department Head then, Professor R. Radhakrishna was a very able agricultural economist who has since had very high-level research and administrative positions at major Indian research and academic institutions. He is one of the most knowledgeable and insightful economists I know working in India today. Professor V.V.N. Somayajulu was a macro-economist and industrial economist, highly skilled in the application of Input-Output Method, which he had at one time studied with Professor Leontief. (I had used that technique for my first work in India.) At Osmania University in the city, Professor J. Mahender Reddy was an Economics faculty member, very knowledgeable in the development policy field. Geeta Gouri, a niece of my old friend K.S. Krishnaswamy, was a very able economist working at one of the research institutes in the city, and very knowledgeable on the economic development of Andhra Pradesh. A former U.N. colleague and friend of mine, Krishna Naidu, had settled near Hyderabad after he left the

U.N. and had set up a commercial farm business there. His knowledge of the region's economy and of business there was very great and very helpful for my work. His wife, Ratna Naidu, was a professor in the University's Sociology Department and has remained a friend after her husband's death.

As part of my grant function, I taught a course in the University's Economics Department and also served on the Ph.D. committee of one of the students, Sunitha Raju, who also was my research assistant. She was very helpful on that research, and we have remained good friends after she got her Ph.D. She later married and moved to Delhi with her husband, where she works with an economic research organization. When we are in Delhi, we try to meet her and her family there.

I met many of the economists in the government and the regional institutes. M. Narasimhan was living in Hyderabad after retiring from the RBI, and had a senior post with one of the major regional institutions, and I very much enjoyed seeing him and exchanging ideas again. He knew well the top economic officials in the state and regions, and his introductions were very helpful. Andhra Pradesh was becoming a center of technological change in India, and I met some of the business leaders introducing those changes. Since my project examined development in other parts of the south, I also visited Kerala, where K.N. Raj, an old friend and a very able economist, headed an economic research institute, to discuss my research with him and his colleagues, two of whom, I. Gulati and his wife, Leela, were also good friends. (Sylvia had known Leela before also.) And of course we visited Madras, one of the South's leading cities for centuries, and the location of the Madras Institute of Development Studies (MIDS), a major research center. It was then headed by Dr. C.T. Kurien, a very able and unorthodox economist educated at Stanford. Sylvia and I became close friends of him and his wife and have remained friends since. During that year, we also met Dr. Vaidyanathan again, who had worked in a variety of major economic positions since we worked together in Bombay in the 1950's. If I remember rightly, he was then in K.N. Raj's Kerala Research Center before moving to the MIDS. He would later head both those research institutes. He was one of the leading agricultural economists in the country, deeply involved in policy-making on rural issues, as well as broader development policies. I learned then that he and Sylvia had been classmates at Cornell and had known each other before I had met him in Bombay in 1955. They were glad to see each other again after many years. He was now married with children, and we enjoyed getting to know his wife and family.

The work I did in India resulted in a book, published in 1988, *Industrial Change in India, 1970-2000*, continuing the title of my first 1958 India book. The American publisher was a good friend of mine, John Adams, himself a leading economist on India, who with his wife, Adele, had established a small publishing company to publish unorthodox economic books. John had been a graduate student of Terry Neale twenty-odd years earlier, and I had been the outsider on his Ph.D. committee. My book was published in India as well. It was a pioneer regional development book on India and well regarded there, but as far as I know has been largely ignored in the United States.

Before Sylvia and I went to India in 1983, UIC had established a faculty exchange relationship with a Chinese university, the Jilin Technical University (JTU) in Changchun in northeastern China. I wanted to go there. I had never been to Communist China though my Ph.D. thesis had discussed China's industrialization. After the death of Mao Zedong and his succession by Deng Xiaoping, China was opened up again for foreign scholars. There was an interest in foreign research and thinking, in addition to investment, as part of that opening. One result of this was such an exchange relationship as the one established between UIC and JTU. I asked Dick Johnson, a good friend and UIC Political Science Professor, then Associate Vice-Chancellor of UIC, if he could arrange an exchange visit there for a month for me on my return from India. This was accepted by JTU, and I was the first UIC faculty invited there. I expected the JTU Management Center would be interested in what I had learned of the Indian economy, since India was a very large neighbor of China, and also industrializing. I of course wanted to learn something of China's development experience and policies.

In fact when I got there in summer 1984, interest in India's industrialization was minimal. I gave one talk on that subject. JTU faculty wanted to get a view of the American economy and of America's potential interest in Chinese industrialization. I spoke on these subjects though I doubt if I was very helpful since I had been out of the U.S. for a year. I wanted to visit some of the Chinese factories in the area, which was being industrialized. I was able to do so with a required guide who was also a translator. One of these was an automobile factory. In those plants I went to I was struck by the large number of workers, the old fashioned work processes and technologies, and the detailed controls over all the work. All the factories were then in the public sector and not profit-oriented. There seemed to be much less flexibility than in the Indian factories I had visited, even those in India's public sector. I myself was welcomed warmly on those visits, and there was real curiosity as to whether American firms might be interested in investing in their production. American firms did in fact invest later in automobile production in the area and elsewhere in China.

Sylvia and I were able to do some sightseeing in the area around Changchun that was enjoyable, in part because one of the younger faculty, Wang Fei, was very helpful and friendly. That guide requirement had been ended by 1986 when we returned, and we found we could travel by ourselves if we wished. In any event we needed a translator. Wang Fei became a good friend. We met his parents, who lived in Changchun, and visited them again in 1987. I helped Wang Fei to come to the U.S. to receive his M.B.A. from UIC, and we have remained in touch in the U.S. and later in China, where he now works for IBM. That month in China was a very interesting addition to our India research year and when we left we hoped we could return for a longer visit fairly soon. Though it was unplanned it turned out we could do that in 1986-1987.

After that month in China, we returned to the United States via Europe. Before we had gone to India, Sylvia had the great idea of applying for a Rockefeller Foundation grant for a month at its Center in Bellagio, Italy, and I applied also. We both got grants, which were to write papers on our year's research work in India. We went to Bellagio in July 1984 and it was a great month there. The Rockefeller Center there was in an old large mansion donated by an Italian family to the Foundation, and on a lovely estate. My office had a beautiful view. When I first saw the office, I wondered if I would be able to work there with such a view, but my writing went very well even with the view – it was a stimulus rather than a deterrent. The meals were great Italian meals, and the company of the other grantees was both enjoyable and stimulating. Another great pleasure was the beautiful location. Bellagio is on Lake Como and we were able to take cruises on the lake, including one to Locarno in Switzerland, where there was the great Thyssen collection of contemporary art. Two of our fellow grantees and their wives, T.J. and Lois Anderson and James and Jane Barr, became life-long friends whom we have seen since then. T.J. Anderson is a musician and composer, who was professor at Tufts and has composed, among other works, a recent opera based on the journal of a black slave in this country before the American Revolution. It is a very powerful work which deserves a wide audience. James Barr was a professor of religious history at Oxford, who after he retired taught in the U.S. and then lived in California near his son. We have seen Lois and T.J. at their home in North Carolina, and on their visits to Chicago and New England. We visited Jane and James at their homes in Oxford and Spain, and more recently in California, and have seen them when they came to Chicago for conferences and visits. The work I did at Bellagio in that month became part of the book eventually published from that year in India.

We returned to Chicago after Bellagio in time for the start of the 1984-1985 academic year at UIC. This was my last full-time teaching year before I retired at age sixty-five in June 1985. This was early retirement, but I was then eligible for my Social Security and University retirement, and Sylvia was still teaching. With my pension income my take-home pay would be about the same as my full-time teaching salary less alimony.

A year after I retired, I was asked by James Riedel, Economics Professor at Johns Hopkins University, if I would be interested in teaching at Nanjing University in China in the first year of the new Johns Hopkins-Nanjing University program. Jim knew of my work in Asia and thought highly of it. That program had recently begun after a friendly American relationship with Communist China had been established at the end of the Vietnam War and Deng Xiaoping's succession to Mao Zedong in China. In this new program Johns Hopkins University would send American faculty to teach in English to Chinese students in different subjects, including Economics, Political Science, History and English Literature. Nanjing University would provide Chinese faculty to teach American and other non-Asian students courses in similar fields on China in Chinese. These would be one year programs; the 1986-1987 program in which I was asked to teach was the first. I told Jim I would be interested, and he told Bill Speidel, the Johns Hopkins Director, who offered me the post. I accepted the offer. Sylvia and I were glad to get it after our month in China in 1984. I thought too I would be able to look at some of the differences in economic development achievements, problems and policies between India and China and possibly write on that when I came back to the U.S. I knew I would not be able to write on that subject in China.

It was a fascinating year. I did not know Chinese, learned a bit to get around, but not enough to carry on lengthy conversations. China was a dictatorship and quite restricted outside the Hopkins-Nanjing Center. I felt in some way as if I were in another world, and for the first time ever I kept a daily journal of my experiences and impressions. If we received any visitor at the Center, whether Chinese or a foreigner, that person had to register at the entrance. After the experiences of the Cultural Revolution when contact with foreigners could be dangerous, and some had been sent to camps for re-education in correct Communism, older Chinese especially were careful of seeming overly friendly with foreigners. Sylvia and I would therefore arrange to meet visitors outside the Center gates if we became friends and met often, so they need not register. We did meet the Chinese faculty, some of whom lived and ate with us at the Center dining room, and that was pleasant. But it was not until late in the year that these Chinese friends invited us to their homes. We were told later they thought we might be upset by their living conditions. But before we left, some faculty had become close friends, spoke to us of their viewpoints and experiences during the Cultural Revolution, invited us to their homes off campus, and gave us lovely gifts when we left.

The Chinese students were very helpful in carrying our bags on joint trips or when we came back. But in class there was almost no discussion. In the Economics courses I taught I tried to get students to speak of economic practices in real life, especially in relation to what I was teaching from the American textbook. I was using Paul Samuelson's text for the Introductory course, which had just been translated in Chinese. It was very difficult to get any examples of how Chinese firms functioned in real life in class. I learned later that the students were afraid that anything they might say in class that appeared critical might be reported to some watch agency, and they could be punished or otherwise harmfully affected. Students did however want to meet the foreign faculty personally, even as friends, and in those one-on-one meetings they often spoke frankly and at times critically of economic practices. In that respect the Chinese students were much different from Indian students who were often openly critical in classes and meetings of business behavior and India's government policies. But many of the Chinese students were very bright and perceptive in their grasp of what I was teaching, and were aware of actual practices and Chinese economic policies and their effects. Some of those students I then taught or knew I later helped gain admission to UIC Graduate College in the Economics program and they have remained friends since. They include Ma Yunxia and Bu Ruizhi, both of whom received UIC graduate degrees and are now living in the United States. The oldest student in that first class was Zhang Yidong, who had been a college teacher before the Cultural Revolution. He had been imprisoned during that time and sent to a camp for re-education. He was released after Deng gained power. His English was quite good and he wrote several articles in English that were later published in American literary journals. He has written an autobiography that I read in manuscript, and I hope is published in the United States.

There were some political demonstrations for greater freedom of expression in Nanjing and some other Chinese cities in 1986-1987, and many students were supportive. Those demonstrations were held in check, but peacefully, without heavy military or police repression and deaths. That may have reflected the strong influence of reform-minded leaders in the Communist Party. Their influence had unfortunately declined before the Beijing Tiannamen Square demonstrations in 1989, which contributed to the violent military response to those demonstrations and the many deaths.

Apart from the pleasures of our interaction with the Chinese faculty members and Chinese students in the program we became close friends with the other American faculty that year. Jim Townsend from the University of Washington taught Political Science. He was a scholar of Chinese history and politics who had lived many years in Hong Kong. He and his wife, Sandy Perry, were very knowledgeable of Chinese history and culture and it was a pleasure to exchange ideas with them. We went to restaurants, music and plays with them in Nanjing and traveled with them to Beijing, Chungking on the Yangtze River, Shanghai and south China. Their command of Chinese, knowledge of the culture and their explanations contributed very much to our appreciation of all of these experiences, and our grasp of Chinese culture. They remained close friends for the rest of their lives until their quite recent and early deaths. Sylvia and I truly miss them.

Bob Fogarty, editor of the *Antioch Review*, taught American history, and his wife, Katherine Kadish, is a very good artist. They were very insightful companions and have remained good friends since, seeing them often in Ohio and Chicago. I am an *Antioch Review* reader, and Bob's own work is very interesting. Katherine established connections with many of Nanjing's art galleries and working artists. Through Bob and Katherine we came in contact with Chinese writers and artists, and we bought some of their art to bring back. We also liked Katherine's own work then and since then and have her paintings and prints she did before and since then.

Dick Gaulton was also teaching political science. He had taught with a leading American university in its China Studies program and was very knowledgeable of China's history and culture. Dick has been our good friend since. Dick later was the American head of the Hopkins program in Nanjing, and he and his future wife, Leslie Eliet, subsequently worked and lived in Chicago before they moved to Cornell and Ithaca, N.Y. Leslie is an artist whose work we like, and we have several of her paintings.

We traveled widely in China and gained both a knowledge and appreciation of Chinese history and culture, and its great contribution to world civilization. We were not there for as long as we were in India, nor did we know the Chinese language, though Sylvia made far more progress than I did. But through our friendships with the Chinese friends we made, and of our American colleagues, especially Jim and Sandy, we gained a sense of the country that we never would have gotten without that year.

I was able to do some economic research also, but that was not my major work. I did want to visit Chinese factories, meet some factory managers, and talk to government economic officials. I was told I would have to get official permission to do this and would need to apply through official channels. I did apply and was not given it – I was told I had not come to China for research, but to teach. This was reversed but only shortly before I was to leave China. Before that change happened I was able to do some factory visits, but unofficially. Chinese friends who knew managers asked them to invite me, and they were interested in my impressions. In talking with some of these managers and local officials I got some sense of the reforms then underway in China; with the greater opening of China to the West they were interested in possible American investment in China. This we know now has occurred on a large scale since the mid-1990's. At the end of that year I thought I might be able to do some work comparing the economic reform process and programs in China after Mao's death in 1980, and in India in the 1980's under Rajiv Gandhi. I was able to go to India on an AIIS grant in 1987-1988 for four months to explore the Indian economic reforms in depth through my many Indian friends who knew India's economic reform issues and policies well. As a product of that year in China and my research in India in 1983-1984 and then 1987-1988, I eventually wrote that book written in part on a Woodrow Wilson Center Fellowship in Washington, D.C., in 1989-1990, and completed at UIC. At UIC my former student at Nanjing, Bu Ruizhi, was my research assistant and most useful as such, and other Chinese students, including Ma Yunxia, another of my Nanjing students, were very helpful. The book *Contrasting Styles of Industrial Reform: China and India in the 1980's* was published in 1992, with the help of Geoffrey Huck, then the Economics editor at the University of Chicago Press, who became a close personal friend during the publication.

I have not mentioned a great additional benefit from that year. On our return from China that summer of 1987 we took the Trans-Siberian Railway from Beijing to Moscow, and we stopped at Irkutsk en route. It was my first time in Russia since I had left it as a three-year-old. I no longer knew any Russian, but it was a fascinating and exciting experience. Siberia was a beautiful country, but it is unlike the highly developed rural mid-west United States that I knew. I thought it was what I imagined the American frontier country must have looked like in the 1880's. On this trip at several of the stops the train made, a group of old women would be waiting at the station near the dining car and the staff of the car would sell them food. There was little better food available for passengers, and we learned early on to go to the local food market in places where we stopped for any length of time to buy food.

Irkutsk was a pleasant city the two days we were there. We visited the local church which was an old one with iconic art work, and the country around the city, which was near Lake Baikal, was attractive. Moscow was a very large city with its Kremlin area more or less sealed from the general public. There were a good many stores in the city selling a variety of consumer products. Lines were long, and I had the impression prices were higher than in China for equivalent items which also seemed less available than in Nanjing. This surprised me, and again made me think that the Soviet Union was not an economic equal of the United States, though it was a great political power then. We also took the train to Leningrad. I wanted to see my birthplace named Petrograd at my birth and today renamed St. Petersburg as before 1917. I recognized nothing there. We visited the Hermitage Museum which had some great art, and Peter the Great's palace and we saw his famous statue. Seeing that city was moving – Tolstoy, Dostoevsky and Pushkin had written about that city. But otherwise the city did not seem in very good physical condition with narrow, old roads and houses that needed repair. The country outside it was attractive. I was lucky that my mother had left Petrograd with me when she did.

From Leningrad we took trains that took us across Europe eventually to Spain for a visit with James and Jane Barr at their summer house near Valencia and to Madrid and Toledo to see the Prado and the great palaces and art. That was a wonderful visit. I would not go to Spain when General Franco ruled Spain. I was glad it has become a democracy, and especially glad we could visit it in 1987. We visited Bilbao and Barcelona in 2001, and I hope very much to visit southern Spain in the near future. Then we returned to the United States with brief stopovers enroute in Paris and London to see friends.

It was a great year and resulted in the book I eventually wrote. During that year, however, there was a very tragic event within my family. My cousin and brother Walter died. He had been diagnosed with cancer before I left for China and death was expected, but not within that year. His death was and is a great personal loss. He had been an elder brother to me, and the family member to whom I had been closest both intellectually and by experience. He had studied Economics before becoming a lawyer. He had worked in government and then gone into academic life. I talked to him of my professional and career interests, and his advice was important for my own decisions and thinking on my ideas and work. And I know he thought highly of me and of my work. We went to see his wife, Nan, when we arrived and saw his three sons, Robert, Dan and Johnny, to express our sorrow.

CHAPTER XI

My Scholarly Life in Chicago After 1978

I N THE PREVIOUS chapter I wrote about my research after I left the Headship of the Economics Department. That was my main reason for coming to UIC, and as that chapter makes clear I was able to do a good deal of research about Chicago, my pre-Chicago experience, and on-going economic development and policy-making in India and China. But I said nothing about my UIC life on the faculty, my life with Sylvia in and near Chicago, nor of Mark and of Sylvia's children as they were growing up. This chapter is about my teaching and my life with my UIC faculty friends after we married.

Within the Department my main job was teaching. I often taught courses in my fields of specialization. Those were in Economic Development and various aspects of Public Policy Analyses, but at times I taught Micro or Macro-Economic courses at the Introductory level. In the graduate Development courses many of those students were from developing countries, especially from Asia. If I were writing about their countries, I would often ask their comments and suggestions, which they were glad to offer and might be useful. Some of the policy analysis courses I gave I would offer jointly with a faculty member in the Political Science or Urban Studies fields on a policy issue we might both have been involved in or studied. That was always interesting for me to get a perspective on a policy issue from a non-economic viewpoint. One such course was on decision-making in non-profit organizations such as universities, and I gave that course with Ron Brady, a top UIC official. Another course was on military decision-making offered with Roger Little who had also served in the Second World War and was a military historian, and I gave a course in the urban development field with Chuck Orlebeke, who had been a top U.S. government official dealing with such problems. I think my students enjoyed those courses. As I mentioned earlier, one of my pleasures after retirement is to be told by a former student about how much he or she got from one of my courses. I have stayed in touch with one of my undergraduate students, David Mathews, who later got an M.B.A. from Northwestern and has worked with business firms in Chicago and the Northeast. I have been in greater contact with my former graduate students, many from Asia, some of whom I taught in China and India and whom I helped to come to UIC, others from those countries and Iran and Bangladesh who were already here. Many of these helped me in my research as assistants or by their comments on my work that they might know about. Thus I enjoyed my teaching although that was not my main interest.

In the Economics Department itself my relation with my colleagues was friendly, though my interest in the work they were doing varied by their fields and my relationships with them. I remained friends with all of those I hired, attended seminars on their work and read their papers if they were not too mathematical for me. I find Joe Persky's urban research and his work on history of economic thought especially interesting, and also Tony Camacho's on enterprise decision-making. Mo Yin Tam, Gib Bassett and Ali Akarca are good friends and I read the papers that they send me, but they are more mathematical than my skills or taste. Of the older faculty who have retired I have stayed in touch with Bill Grampp who lives nearby and whose work I enjoy, but seem to have lost touch with Elie Ayal and Oscar Miller. I had enjoyed

Elie's development work, but haven't seen any for some years. Of other faculty who were at UIC when I came I am friends with Dick Kosobud, Houston Stokes and John McDonald when we meet in the campus hallways, but don't have much contact in our work – they are far more mathematically oriented than I am and always have been. They have made major contributions in their fields, but they are usually beyond my understanding.

Dick and Houston were most helpful to me when they were department heads. Dick, my successor, gave me research leave for my UIC location project and for the one on the Harvard and MIT advisory experiences in India and Pakistan. He also introduced me to Manoranjan Dutta, at Rutgers, also a student of Lawrence Klein. Jan Dutta had founded the American Committee On Asian Economic Studies (ACAES) and the *Journal of Asian Economics* (JAE), which he edits. He is not only a very able and productive economist, but the most effective academic entrepreneur I have known. I am very happy I met him and his wife, who are good friends, through Dick. Houston followed Dick as Department Head and granted me leave for my 1983-1984 India project. He was responsible for handling my 1985 retirement application and supported that request and my Emeritus Professor appointment which was most useful for my relations with UIC after 1985.

Of the faculty who were hired after I left the Headship I've been very friendly with Evelyn Lehrer on both a social and professional level. She had studied at Northwestern and was hired by Dick. Her economic work on Human Capital and the Economics of Religion interest me, and I like her very much as a person. The two faculty who were hired by Dick with whom I have been most in contact for professional reasons are Barry and Carmel Chiswick. I had tried to hire Barry on Jagdish Bhagwati's suggestion when I was Head. He had been at Columbia after getting his Ph.D., but I didn't succeed. Dick did succeed in hiring both Barry and Carmel. I had not made an offer to Carmel when I made the offer to Barry, and I believe that error was why Barry didn't come earlier. In any event I'm glad Carmel did join the Department. She is a very able development economist who has worked in Thailand among other countries. She has been doing interesting work also in the Economics of Religion, examining how changing economic forces have influenced religious practice. Barry Chiswick had also gone to Brooklyn College and it turned out that I had met Carmel's father, Morris Ullman, a distinguished economist, in Washington years before. I find Barry's work on immigration very interesting, and his work was a stimulus to my decision to write my autobiography on this theme. Another more recent addition to the Department who is a personal friend is Richard Peck. I had known his father, Merton Peck, at RAND when he visited there while he was at Yale on the economics faculty. Richard had received his Ph.D. at Princeton and I find his work of interest though more mathematical than I enjoy. He has also been working for the World Bank on different social problems in developing countries and that of course interests me.

Recently Deidre McCloskey joined the UIC faculty on an interdisciplinary appointment in Economics, History and English. She is doing most interesting work in Economic History, philosophy and methodology. We have become good friends though I've long retired, and it is a pleasure to get to know her personally, beyond her work that I've always enjoyed. She is a person of great courage and has written a fascinating book on her decision to change from a male to a female. I spent several days with her in Amsterdam recently, where I had not been since I was three years old, when I left Russia with my mother. Deidre was teaching there for the term. I had not realized how beautiful that canal city is. Larry Officer was also hired after I was Head. He had been at Michigan State University where he was a good friend of Subbiah Kannappan. I find his work interesting, and we have been friends with him and Sandra since he joined. In the faculty I hired, Mo Yin, Joe and Tony are among my and Sylvia's closest personal friends in Chicago. We meet often socially with them and their spouses, Shiu Wing, Vicky and Victoria. I am also in close touch with Jackie Moses, Ron's widow, whose art I like very much, and whom we always enjoy meeting.

When I was Department Head, Geri Kennedy was a great assistant. She left the Department sometime after I left as Head, and was followed during the period before I retired by Lynn Lacy and her assistant Yvonne Curtis. They were very supportive both for my teaching and my research needs before and after I retired. They themselves recently retired or left, and were followed by Carol Martell who is very helpful. I consider all of them not only assistants but after my formal retirement as friends whom I am very glad I know personally. We meet socially and talk freely about things we enjoy in common.

While they were at UIC, I had known Fran Flanagan, now Fran Van Loo, Woody Bowman, Millie Marnin, Mike McPherson and Will White well, and enjoyed their Economic work as well as personal friendship. Woody, now married to Michele Thompson, and Millie now work elsewhere, but live in Chicago and we meet often as friends. Fran, Will and Mike live far from Chicago. I've lost touch with Mike, but keep in touch with and try to see Fran and Will and their spouses whenever I have been near Berkeley or New Haven. On my 80th birthday Joe and Mo Yin gave a party for me at Joe and Vicky's home in Chicago. I had expected a small affair, but it was a surprise larger party to which most of the Department faculty and staff came and spoke of their memories of me, and there were messages from former faculty. I was deeply touched by the warmth and friendship at that party.

So far I have talked of my relationships within the Economics Department. In the CBA after I left as Head, I remained a good friend of Irv Heckman's successor as Dean, Ralph Westfall. As I've already mentioned, he was very supportive of my research, and interested in my India work since he had spent a year there. We have remained good friends with him and Charlotte even after we retired. Bob Weigand is my closest friend from among my colleagues in the College outside the Department.

In the UIC campus community as a whole, Lore Segal in the English Department became Sylvia's and my closest friend. She was teaching Creative Writing – and we met her through Robie Macauley who was also living in Chicago then. Sylvia and I had then moved to Chicago near the UIC campus, and Lore also moved into that same apartment in the early '80s. Lore's permanent residence was and is in New York, and she came to Chicago for about four days a week during the term to teach. She was a widow, with her mother and children living with her, and with many friends and literary colleagues in New York and she wanted to stay there. We shared Chicago apartments until she left UIC about fifteen years later. Living with her was a great pleasure then, and we have remained life-long friends. She visited us when we were in

Nanjing and later in India. She was a child refugee from Austria in the 1930's after Hitler took power there, then lived in England during the war before coming to the U.S. via Latin America soon after the war. Fortunately her parents were able to get to England also just before September 1939 and the start of the war. Her novels and memoirs of her leaving Austria, life in England, and settling in the United States and living here are both fascinating and very enjoyable. She is an excellent guide to past European literature, and to work by contemporary authors of the U.S. and around the world. She has great taste in contemporary art and theatre, and it's always a pleasure to be with her.

It was essentially through Lore that Sylvia and I got to know our closest Chicago friends, outside our departments, who are at UIC now. They are John Huntington and his wife, Virginia Wexman. Both are Professors in the English Department – John teaches Shakespeare and H.G. Wells, among others. Virginia teaches film, and Sylvia has taught courses with her on Indian film. John and Virginia live near us in Chicago, and we meet often at their place, where they show movies regularly. We have traveled with them on their foreign trips on which they have invited us. Virginia is a great travel arranger. We have been with them in Mexico several times and in Europe in London and Paris and most recently on a most enjoyable week in Crete. They are great companions not only on travel, but in Chicago as well going with us to plays, movies and restaurants.

I had also seen Robie and Anne regularly while they lived in Chicago. Anne died in the mid-1980's. She had been a good friend and her death was a personal loss for me. Some years later Robie married Pam Painter, a young writer whom Sylvia and I also enjoy knowing. Sometime after their marriage, Robie had retired from *Playboy* (he was older than I was), and he and Pam moved to Boston where they had a house. We stayed in close touch, seeing each other every summer when we were in New England, until Robie died a few years ago. He had been one of my oldest friends going back to our Bard years together in the late 1940's, and his death was a real personal loss – I had gained so very much by knowing him. We have seen Pam during the summers since then, when she comes to her place on Cape Cod, or in Boston.

Manuel and Elfriede Blanco-Gonzalez were other good friends from literature, Manuel in Spanish, until his very recent death. We hope to continue to see Elfriede who decided to remain in the Chicago area, rather than move to Florida as they had both planned to do before Manuel died.

Two good friends from the Art Department are Marty Hurtig and Leon Bellin. Marty's wife, Anita, worked in the Medical School before retiring, and Leon's wife, Norma, had been in the campus administration. Marty is an excellent abstract artist whose work I very much like and we have some. We see Marty and Anita often, visiting art galleries with them and going to operas and plays together. Leon and Norma, like me, had gone to Brooklyn College as undergraduates. After Leon and Norma retired and moved out west, we see them much less often. I like Leon's art, which is not abstract, and we have some.

Another one of my good friends, associated with my UIC background during much of the 1980's, was Mimi Singer. Her husband, Rolf, had been one of the leading world mycologists. He was associated with a major Chicago research institute in that field, and was on the UIC faculty. She was an artist, whose work I liked very much. He was about twenty years older than I was, and Mimi about ten years older. He died some years after we met, and Mimi became a close friend as a widow. I forget how we had first met – it may have been through the Blanco-Gonzalezes, who also lived in the northern suburbs then, or Jackie Moses, a fellow artist and close friend of both of us who painted Mimi's portrait and gave that to Sylvia and myself after her death.

Rolf had been a scientist in Germany before Hitler, and had been associated with anti-Nazi movements before 1933. Fortunately they were able to leave in the 1930's for Russia, China and Japan, when he received research grants for work in those countries. They had crossed Europe and Asia by train before 1939. If I remember rightly, they were in Japan during its war with the United States. After the war, they moved to Argentina, and he did major biological research there and in Brazil and neighboring countries. They came to Chicago in the late 1950's or 1960's on his major research appointment. Mimi was a very stimulating, broad-minded, German-educated intellectual and artist. After her husband's death, she lived as an active widow in the attractive apartment they had in Evanston. It was always enjoyable to visit with her there to exchange ideas and see her art, and we might meet in Chicago for art shows and concerts. After a stroke in her late years, she moved to California to be near her daughter living near San Diego. We saw her there, on our visits to Arna, before she died several years ago.

My speaking of friends on the UIC faculty will end the part of the chapter that focuses on my direct UIC experience, except for this one related matter. I was struck by the very little interest that UIC faculty had in organizing to improve their work conditions and salaries. I had always supported labor unions when that was appropriate, and when I joined the faculty, I became a member of the Association of American University Professors (AAUP) at the suggestion of Bill Grampp. As Department Head, I could not be active in it, but I wanted to show my support. It was and is quite influential on the Urbana campus in influencing policy with respect to faculty there. It was never popular or influential among UIC faculty before I retired from the faculty, or since, though in recent years both John Huntington and Joe Persky are active members of the UIC chapter and have been taking strong steps to recruit more faculty members and influence the administration. I hope they will be successful so that UIC faculty may gain benefits Urbana faculty have gained.

After my Headship, I also joined the American Federation of Teachers (AFT) because it seemed to be able to influence the Illinois state administration and legislature on university issues, thinking too it might attract more faculty members than the AAUP did on campus. It is quite strong in the state colleges, and on matters affecting the staff in the University, but not the faculty. Its political strength reflects its national union position. It has little appeal to UIC faculty. I don't know the reasons for the low appeal of the AAUP at UIC in contrast to Urbana, nor the lack of appeal of the AFT. I personally think that indifference has not helped the welfare of the faculty at UIC.

Outside the UIC I was also actively involved in various scholarly activities. In Chicago I was in close touch with the University of Chicago's South Asia program, and I am still a formal associate of that program. It is one of the country's leading South Asia programs, and by my association with it I am in contact with University of Chicago scholars in that field other than economists, and with visitors from other schools and from India, participating in that program. By my formal relationship I also have access to University of Chicago's excellent library and other facilities. As mentioned, I knew the University's leading economists who worked on Indian economic development and development elsewhere, met them, and we talked about each other's research in progress, and opinions. As I mentioned, Bert Hoselitz had been a good friend for many years. When he decided to retire as Editor of *Economic Development and Cultural Change* (EDCC), a pioneer journal in that field, he asked me if I would be interested in succeeding him. I told him I would be – I was honored by his idea. He suggested my name to the University of Chicago Economics Faculty, but Gale Johnson, one of that University's leading faculty, was also interested. Understandably Gale, who had been on that faculty for many years, was selected. Gale asked me if I would be interested in being Book Editor. I told him I would be and I became that. I was Book Editor of EDCC for over fifteen years, starting from about 1987 when I came back from China, and I enjoyed that very much. Gale was a great person to work with, and in effect he gave me the power under his broad authority to choose the books we reviewed, choose the reviewers, and make decisions on the reviews. I of course asked his suggestions and he offered them himself. He also became a close friend with whom I would exchange ideas on my work, on the Indian economy which I knew well, on China which he knew very well, and on broader development policies. I also got to know well as an associate and friend, Lea Green, who was the Managing Editor of the journal, and had been so when Bert was editor. She handled all the administrative tasks involved in editing the journal and did an excellent job. Apart from that she became a very good friend. She is very interested in art and theatre, and I very much enjoyed talking to her about these. She left her Managing Editor work before I ended my Book Editing and was succeeded by Kathryn Kraynick who did a fine job in the years before Gale left Chicago and his recent death. Gale's death is a loss to the Economics profession, and the personal loss of a friend. With his death the EDCC had gone through the process of finding a successor to Gale; the one selected has moved from one university not far from Chicago to another in California. Kathryn left as Managing Editor as a result of those shifts in location of the journal.

I have been closely associated too with Jan Dutta as a Board member and Treasurer of the ACAES for some years and being on the editorial board of the *Journal of Asian Economics* (JAE). I have attended ACAES conferences where I've given papers and chaired sessions on relevant economic issues. Two of those were in Bangkok and Tokyo, where I enjoyed seeing old friends and work associates, including some former students now living and working in those cities. I have also suggested articles for the JAE and reviewed submissions for it. I see Jan when I am in New York, and have visited him and his wife, Kanak, at their home near New Brunswick. Kanak is a most interesting woman who is a significant figure in the New Jersey Democratic party, contributing to the election of an Indian-American to the state legislature from her district. Jan has been an advisor on state and national economic policy to Democratic Party administrations and on Indo-American issues in U.S. Census and immigration work. They are living evidence of the major contribution of contemporary immigrants to American society.

On my Woodrow Wilson Center Fellowship in Washington, D.C., for four months in 1989-1990 Sylvia and I lived near DuPont Circle, and I went daily to the Center then near the National Gallery of Art (formerly the Mellon). Washington had changed greatly since the 1950's as it became a great national city rather than the small southern town it had been when I worked there in the early 1950's. I saw many old friends who lived in or near there. Jack and Marion Carroll, Len and Flor Felsenthal and Peter and Mary Kay Muncie all were nearby and we met often at their homes or in town. Prasenjit Duara, an historian working on China, was also a Woodrow Wilson Fellow then, and I enjoyed meeting him there. He has since joined the University of Chicago. The director of the Center's Asia program, Mary Brown Bullock, was an expert on Chinese history and politics and was both very helpful in my work and very stimulating in her ideas. We became good friends and have kept in touch every so often. I gave a talk at the Center on my India-China project and comments were useful from other fellows and from the scholars in the Washington area who came to the talk. And of course I visited the Johns Hopkins University School for Advanced International Studies (SAIS) in Washington where the American office of the Hopkins-Nanjing Center was located. I met Bill Speidel and Jim Riedel again to exchange ideas on my research and to renew friendships, and I enjoyed that. Francis Shieh, from RAND, now had an academic post in Maryland and it was a pleasure to see him again and talk about China, which he visited often, and our work. An added pleasure was that in the time I was on the fellowship Ian Little was briefly visiting the World Bank. His 70th birthday was during that visit. His local friends had a large birthday party for him and that was most pleasant. His wife, Dobs, whom I had first met in India in 1958 had not come to the U.S. for Ian's short visit. One or two years later she died so I did not see her again. She was someone whom I had liked whenever we met, and I was sorry for Ian. Several years later Ian met Lydia Segrave and they married and I have visited them at Oxford when I'm in England. She is a sculptress and I like her personally and her work, and Ian is lucky to have found her.

A great pleasure of those months in Washington was that Sylvia and I visited Walter's son, Dan, and his wife, Leslie Maitland, there. Dan worked with Jim Lehrer then, as he does now, and Leslie was a "New York Times" correspondent there. While we had met each other frequently for short occasions, this was our first lengthy get-together. They have a lovely place outside of the city itself, and then two very young children. It was a great pleasure to get to catch up with Dan, whom I had always thought highly of, to exchange ideas, to learn what he was doing with respect to the Jim Lehrer program, and to hear about his brothers. Leslie was very knowledgeable of Washington and very intelligent, and it was great to talk to her. We learned too that she was a University of Chicago graduate. We saw her later in Chicago, and Zachary, their son, started as an undergraduate there in September 2004. We live in Hyde Park near that University now and see him often, and hope to see his father, mother and sister when they visit him.

In this chapter I have told about my friendships while in Chicago, associated with UIC and my research, but I have said nothing yet of my family: of my wife of the past twenty-five years who has made this such a happy period of my life and of my life with her; my son, Mark, who matured over those years, and Sylvia's four children whom she had raised who also matured, and who lived with both of us for some years. The next two chapters will be of that part of my life.

CHAPTER XII

Living with Sylvia in Chicago

B EFORE WE MARRIED, Sylvia and I had been living at her home in Evanston for about a year, and we continued to live there after our marriage. Sylvia had four children ranging in age from Sanjaya the oldest, born in 1958, to Jaidev the youngest, born only five years later in 1963. Two daughters, Arna and Sunita, were born in 1959 and 1961. She returned to the U.S. with Ved soon after Sanjaya's birth in London, and raised all of them when married to Ved. At the same time she was getting her Ph.D. at Harvard, teaching in California, and doing research in India before coming to the Anthropology Department at UIC in 1970. It obviously could not have been easy for her.

Three of Sylvia's children were working and going to school in Chicago and Evanston in 1980. Sanjaya had finished the technical education he wanted and was working with Eastman Kodak in the area. Arna was working in a local business office and was studying at UIC for an undergraduate degree in Accounting. Jai was finishing Evanston high school and playing in local rock bands. Sunita had entered the University of California at Berkeley when she finished high school and was living there, visiting us between terms. The three children in the Chicago area lived with us and our two cats until Jai finished High School. The biggest family event of the years we all lived together was the birth of Arna's son, Dallas, in 1982. Arna was not living with Dallas' father then. She wanted to have the birth at home with a midwife attending. She had the birth under the midwife's care at the house. The birth went well and Dallas was born in fine health. Sylvia was of course very helpful during the birth and taking care of Arna and Dallas both before and after, until Arna was up again. It was for me a very moving experience, and the closest I have ever been to watching a live birth. I had not seen Mark's actual birth in the Boston hospital where he was born.

While I was living in Evanston with Sylvia and her children, Mark was studying at Lawrence College in Wisconsin and living there. Between terms he lived with Kusum, first in Wilmette in the house which was hers after our divorce, and then in the apartment she lived in after she had sold that house. When he finished college with a B.A. in Economics, he worked in the area Baskin-Robbins stores in managerial positions for several years before deciding to enter John Marshall Law School in Chicago for a law degree. Kusum financed his law degree education to the extent necessary since she now owned all our former joint property and received half my salary. I saw Mark quite often, usually with Sylvia and at times with Sylvia's children. I also tried to see Kusum about once a month if she could use my help, but she handled her affairs herself. She later decided to move to Florida where she has been living for many years.

After Jai graduated from High School, he decided to go to the University of Wisconsin at Madison for his college education. Sometime after he started there and after Dallas' birth, Sylvia thought that we no longer needed to continue to live in Evanston, an hour or more from UIC, and that we might move closer to the campus. I thought it was a good idea. She also thought it would be especially pleasant to live in the country rather than in Chicago on weekends when we were not teaching, while renting an apartment close to campus to live in during our teaching days. I had mixed feelings about that idea, never having lived in the country, but I was willing to try it. Sylvia would have the money for the country house after she sold her Evanston house.

We did find a house and thirteen acres of land in the rural country just outside of Lake Geneva, Wisconsin. This had been part of a much larger farm going back to a Swiss immigrant family that had settled there before the Civil War. The present owner, of that family, Harold Meyerhofer and his wife, Jean, were now in the cattle raising and dairy farming business, requiring much less land. They lived in their own home across the road from the land and house they sold us. Sylvia sold her Evanston house and took a mortgage on the Lake Geneva property, and we moved there. We also rented a small apartment in the Italian neighborhood just west of UIC and moved there with Lore Segal. Lake Geneva is about seventy-five miles from the UIC campus area and downtown Chicago (the Loop), about an hour and a half drive. It was a great decision. During the week while we were teaching, we could enjoy the many cultural activities in and near the Loop. The Art Institute, Symphony Hall, Lyric Opera, the Music of Baroque and many theatres were near us, and of course UIC had many academic and cultural events. On weekends and between quarters we lived in Wisconsin which was now our voting residence. The country we lived in was beautiful and our thirteen acres were great for walking during fall and spring, and for cross-country skiing, which we did in the winter snow. It was a completely new experience for me with my Bridgeport and Brooklyn growing up. For Sylvia, who had been raised on a farm in Rhode Island, it was a return to a life she had once enjoyed. She now was able to plant berries and other fruits; we ate them fresh and off the vine as well as at our table. Our neighbors, the Meyerhofers, were very friendly. We enjoyed talking with them and they were very valuable guides to the pleasures of the area. Lake Geneva was not far from our home, only a short ride. There were several very pleasant restaurants overlooking the lake and ceramic studios making pottery nearby. The move from Evanston was a great idea of Sylvia's. While we were living there, we invited members of our departments to come up on weekends for parties or for individual visits, and they enjoyed that. We lived there for about ten years. In the early 1990's Lake Geneva was becoming a more suburbanized part of the wider Chicago region and was less attractive to us. We were also buying Sylvia's aunt's house on Cape Cod about that time and could use the money, so we sold that house then. We try to visit Lake Geneva every so often to see Jean Meyerhofer who lives in her family house, and to buy pottery. It is more or less on the way to Mark and Kymberlee's home north of Milwaukee, about which more later.

I had mentioned earlier that we had bought a summer place in Bristol, Rhode Island, off Narragansett Bay before we were married. We spent our summers there – it was right on the water and we could go in for a swim before breakfast which was very enjoyable. We had bought it also because it was near Middletown and Newport. Sylvia had been born and raised in the family house in Middletown before going to Cornell. Her mother and father lived in that house. It was not far from Bristol, and we saw them often, going with them to the neighboring Newport beaches and restaurants and to concerts and other events in Newport. I had never seen the old Newport mansions of the Vanderbilts and others built after the 1870's. These are architecturally interesting, contain art by major artists, and have spectacular sea-fronts and estate grounds. But the greatest pleasure of those summer visits was to meet Sylvia's parents. Her father, Christopher Dutra, was a practicing architect, trained at Rhode Island School of Design (RISD) in contemporary architecture working as an independent architect and later for the state. He designed the house in Falmouth in which I am writing this. His father and mother had come from the Azores Islands, part of Portugal, in the second half of the 19th century. His father first worked as a farm laborer for one of the Rhode Island farm families, then bought his own land for cultivating and home for residence that his son lived in and his granddaughter, my wife, grew up in. He was one of the early Portuguese immigrants to the U.S. who migrated to Rhode Island and Massachusetts as farmers and settled here, and raised later generations. Portuguese immigration to the U.S. continues today and is a significant contribution to New England's society and economy. His son, Chris, married Dorothea Pyne, descended from Irish immigrants to Boston after the mid-19th century Irish rebellion had been crushed by the English. Dorothea and her sister Ruth had college educations, and Chris met his future wife at RISD. She was not only Chris' wife and mother of three daughters, but she later studied nursing and worked as a nurse in New England. I was very glad to be able to meet Sylvia's parents, and even more to get to know them before they died.

I also met Sylvia's aunt, Ruth, who had a home in Falmouth on a lovely Buzzards Bay location. Chris designed that house, in which she lived for many years while she taught in schools in other parts of the state, and after she retired. After the Second World War, she had worked in Japan on Okinawa during the American Occupation, which she found very interesting and collected some lovely Japanese art work. Since I had also worked in Japan for the State Department a bit later, I enjoyed meeting and talking to her about that. We were delighted to get her offer of her house which Sylvia accepted, both because her house was lovely itself and because we had been looking for another house in the area in place of our Bristol house. Sylvia sold that Bristol house and with the proceeds from that sale and the Lake Geneva sale bought Ruth's Falmouth home, taking out a mortgage that would provide Ruth a long-term income flow. We've lived in the Falmouth house for our summers ever since. Originally we thought we might live there year round after we both retired from UIC, but we like Chicago too much to move from there.

Sylvia's younger sister Judy lived in Medway, Massachusetts, about half way between Cape Cod and Boston. She and Sylvia were very close when they were growing up. She was a musician, had studied at The New England Conservatory and was an organist and teacher of music in the area where she lived. She just died of cancer on the last day of 2004. I had known her since 1978, we saw each other often every summer, and she became a sister to me. Her husband, Gary, whom I met a bit later, is like a brother, a very good friend with whom I feel very close whenever we meet.

Sylvia's youngest sister, Linda, had been living in California when Sylvia and I married. We had met a few times until she and Dave, her husband, moved to Middletown in 1996. Linda took over the Dutra home there shortly after Chris died. We now see each other every summer, and I feel she is a close friend, as is Dave, though we meet him less often. They recently moved to Maine to be near children, and sold the old family home.

During our summers in Bristol and Falmouth, I also met Sylvia's former brother-in-law, Ken Hunnibell, who had been Linda's first husband and who taught at Rhode Island School of Design (RISD) in Providence. Sylvia had remained friends with him and his second wife, Sherrill, and we would meet every so often. They lived in Rehoboth, not far from Providence. Ken and Sherrill lived next door to one of my oldest friends from my India work in the mid-1950's, Morris D. Morris, who was doing historical research there then. He and his wife, Michelle McAlpin, had bought a house next to Ken's after Morris came to Brown University from the University of Washington. Ken died a year ago; Sherrill still lives there and is an artist, teaching at a nearby college. I very much like her abstract art work, and we have some of her paintings, and we see her in the summer. We also try to see Morris and Michelle every summer.

Children of Judy's and Linda's live in New England not very far from us, and we see some of them and their spouses every year at their or their mothers' homes. They have their own careers and lives, and I enjoy talking to them when we do meet. Judy's daughter Colleen is an actress whom we've enjoyed seeing in plays. We celebrated, with her husband, John, her parents and brother, Ted, and his wife, Anne, the birth of her daughter in November 2004. Linda's daughter, Meredith, and Pai Lin, her lovely young daughter of a Thai father, have lived very near to Linda, and we have seen them often. Linda's other daughters have lived nearby and we enjoy seeing them, though that is less often.

Once we decided to live full-time during the term in Chicago, we bought an apartment near the campus. That area had begun to go upscale by the mid-1980's, which was somewhat later than the area's businessmen had hoped when the UIC campus was built in the 1960's. We found a two-bedroom apartment with a study room a few blocks west of the campus, off Taylor Street, which was the center of the Italian area. It has top-notch Italian restaurants and groceries and is not far from the city's best Greek restaurants and the Loop.

I have mentioned in the previous chapter that Lore Segal had shared our rented apartment, and she also joined us in the apartment we then bought. The UIC Librarian, Beverly Lynch, had also shared our previous rented apartment when she was in Chicago – she and her husband, John, had a home in Milwaukee – and we became close friends and colleagues. She left for UCLA for a position there in about 1990; John had left his Milwaukee law practice before then and they moved to the Los Angeles area. Beverly's work brings her to Chicago periodically and we see her then, and they have both visited us in Falmouth. They are good friends we are glad we got to know well through sharing a place with Beverly.

Several close friends of Sylvia's at UIC with whom I became friends, are Bhama Srinivasan and Judy Gardiner, both neighbors of ours when we lived near the campus. Bhama is a Math professor who is of the same family as Sylvia's close friends and research associates in Madras. Judy is in the English Department. She is a close friend and former colleague of Lore's, and of course of John and Virginia's today. We often go to Chicago concerts and operas with Bhama or Judy, both of whom enjoy music as much as we do. We have often visited Bhama's cousin, T. Krishnan, and his wife, Janaki, who live in Madras, whenever we are there. They are very knowledgeable of events in Madras and India. Sylvia of course knows many faculty members in anthropology and other Liberal Arts departments at UIC, and I've had the pleasure of getting to know them through her. Sona Hoisington, who headed the Russian Department at UIC, translated letters my mother had written before she came with me to America. Helen had only found them recently among some of the old papers my mother had left in Bridgeport after she died. Sona did that as a favor that I very much appreciated. We have seen Sona this past summer – she and her husband live on Cape Cod after her retirement from UIC. Sylvia has of course many professional colleagues in the University of Chicago's Anthropology Department in the South Asia program. Today I think none of the U of Chicago economists work in or on South Asia. I learn of the interesting visitors, including scholars who come and talk there who are not economists, mainly through Sylvia. We attend many of those talks, which are often stimulating and informative.

At UIC my own greatest pleasures today are the concerts. Almost every Tuesday afternoon there is a concert. I go to almost all those whenever I'm in Chicago, and since I am retired I can go. One of the benefits of attending those concerts, apart from the music itself, is that I've gotten to know Ted Edel, the Music Professor who arranges the concerts, who has become a good friend. He is himself an excellent pianist, and I very much enjoy going to his own concerts, at UIC or elsewhere in Chicago. Like Sylvia and me, Ted was a friend of Jim Hartnett and his wife, Edith. Jim was a Professor of Electrical Engineering at UIC before he retired and is still active on campus. I had known him for many years through joint committee work when we had first met, and later I met his wife, Edith, a psychologist working in Chicago. Edith had a New York upbringing like myself, and we struck it off well. The four of us became good friends, going to concerts and plays in the city. Jim often went with me to the Tuesday afternoon concerts where we also met Ted. Edith died about five years ago, and that was a personal loss to me – she had been someone I was always glad to meet. Jim and I meet several times each year since her death, usually to go together to the Tuesday concerts. But communication is difficult with his speech, and my hearing problem, so we don't meet as often as we once did when Edith was alive.

Dick Johnson, who was Head of the Political Science Department and Vice-Chancellor of UIC, and Karen Egerer, his wife, are good friends of both Sylvia and myself. Sylvia of course knew Dick since they were both in the Liberal Arts College. I had met him from my interest in policy analysis, and as I mentioned he had been responsible for our 1984 month in China. Karen had worked in the UIC International Affairs office, and then set up her own consulting firm which has done work for the U.S. government, aid agencies and private firms in different developing countries, so I got to know her on her own quite well. Sylvia and I have many mutual interests with both of them, and they too enjoy music and theatre. Karen's son Paul's birthday is the same as mine so we often celebrate together. We visit their home in Chicago and vice versa – and they have been able to come to Falmouth in the summer several times.

Among our best non-academic friends in the city are Julie and Ralph Walsh, the owners of the Walsh Art Gallery in Chicago. They are a young couple who established the first art gallery in Chicago that specialized in contemporary Asian art. They opened their gallery about twenty years ago. I became friends with them because Julie remembered I was one of the few people who came to the gallery's opening, which I had seen announced in the paper. Until the late 1990's the gallery had concentrated on Chinese, Japanese and Korean contemporary artists, or American artists influenced by Asian art traditions or experience. Since the late 1990's, they have also shown art by Indian, Pakistani and other South Asian artists, and Americans influenced by those styles. Sylvia and I are very interested in their art shows and see them whenever we are in town. We had introduced Katherine Kadish to them, and Katherine had a show of her work there, since that had been influenced by her experience in China. Another UIC faculty member who goes to Walsh Gallery openings often is Woodman Taylor, who teaches Indian art in the Art History Department. Woodman and his wife, Molshree, are good friends whom we enjoy knowing. She is the daughter of Dr. J.C. Sharma, formerly India's consul-general in Chicago, who became a good friend when there and still is.

We have many friends outside of Chicago as well. I have already spoken of many whom I had met through my research. I have not mentioned the large number whom Sylvia had known through her work and life and with whom I became close friends after we married. When she had been at Cornell, she roomed with Ditta Silberman for a year, and they remained good friends. Ditta has taught in New York and lives in the city. We often stay with her, and she visits us in Falmouth. She is an interesting person to be with and to exchange ideas.

Owen Lynch is one of this country's leading anthropologists working on India, and has been teaching at NYU. He has done important research in India of course, especially on issues of caste. He and Sylvia have much in common in their interests, and I enjoy talking to him. We try to see him when we are in New York, and if one of us goes into the city Sylvia or I may be able to stay in his apartment; I did that very recently.

He often visits us in Falmouth when we are there, and we always enjoy our exchanges.

Pauline Kolenda was at Cornell and working on India when Sylvia was there. They have remained close friends since then and see each other often. She may be Sylvia's closest friend among American anthropologists today. I remember I met her while I was with the MIT Center, but I didn't know her or her work very well. Terry Neale had known her well and thought very highly of her work. After my marriage to Sylvia, I became a good friend of hers and visited her and her husband in Texas when they were living there before he died. We see each other often now in many places when her and Sylvia's paths cross.

Sylvia has many other anthropologist and social science friends who had been and are still working in India. Several of these are in Europe, in England and France, as well as in this country. When we are in London, we often stay with Chris Fuller, Anthropology Professor at the LSE, and his wife, Penny, a solicitor, who have a very pleasant house in the Herne Hill area where Ruskin had once lived. I enjoy those visits very much – they are both good friends. Likewise Pat and Lionel Caplan, now retired Professors at other leading London institutions, who live in North Finchley in the north London area, whom I like very much. Sylvia's research requires her to spend lengthy periods in England working in India Office Records in archives in London. We spent one summer in the apartment that Maurice and Taya Zinkin then had in the Kensington district (it was in the same building as T.S. Eliot's old apartment). They were away from London for that summer. In another summer we were in the home of Adrian Mayer, one of England's leading anthropologists on India, who had been Sylvia's teacher when she studied in London. That house was in Highgate, a very pleasant area of the city. I always enjoy visits to London, one of the world's greatest cities. It has some of the world's best theatres, orchestras and art museums and excellent book shops. I have my own personal friends who live or lived near there whom I've mentioned in earlier chapters – Ian Little, Scarlett Epstein, the Zinkins before they died, and Miriam Gunesekera. I would try to visit them with Sylvia if that were possible given her work schedule, or alone.

Sylvia had other close colleagues and friends in Edinburgh, Pat and Roger Jeffrey, Professors at the University of Edinburgh. They have invited us to stay with them at their very pleasant home in the city. I like them very much personally, and I was very glad to go to Edinburgh. I think it's one of the most attractive cities I have been in. It has a beautiful scenic view, a very interesting history with historic buildings I enjoy visiting, and a very good museum. It also has good plays and concerts, especially in the summer concert period which we have sometimes overlapped.

Another close long-time friend of Sylvia's is Eva Lambert, whom she had met on a cross-Atlantic voyage. Eva and her husband live on Skye Island off Scotland. We have visited them several times. That is one of the world's loveliest places that I know, though it has become more of a tourist center since our first visit. Eva's husband is a commercial fisherman, with his own boat, fishing off the island. Eva and he raise sheep on their land and sell the wool. We enjoy our trips there very much. On one of those trips to reach Skye we drove from London, first crossing England via the old Roman road and Hadrian's castle, to Edinburgh, where we stayed with Pat and Roger. We then crossed Scotland to Skye. The countryside was lovely in the good weather we had, and it was a very pleasant and interesting drive. Eva's son Aaron is now working for his Ph.D. at the University of Chicago, and we see him in the city.

An anthropologist friend who worked in India over the years is at Brown University in Providence. Lina Fruzetti is a very interesting scholar born in Ethiopia who did research in Africa and in India. Her husband, Akos Ostor, teaches at Wesleyan, and is a documentary film maker as well as an anthropologist, working in India's villages. We have seen several of their documentaries which present very insightful pictures of life and social relationships in the villages where he has worked. They are good friends and Providence is not far from our summer home. The fact that Akos is from Hungary and Lina from Ethiopia makes them even more interesting beyond our common India experiences. Akos kept in touch with friends during the Communist rule and has visited Hungary since and we can talk about those years. Lina has memories of the Italian rule in Ethiopia and Haile Selassie's rule after that. I know very little of Africa and learn through what she tells us.

Sylvia's own research took her to India in the 1980's and 1990's. In the 1980's we usually went together, she getting her individual grant and I mine. In the 1990's I was no longer applying, and I accompanied her on her grants. Her work was largely in South India, in Hyderabad and Madras. We would always spend several weeks in Delhi where she met leading Indian social scientists and anthropologists, some of whom I knew from my work. One of these mutual friends is Professor T.N. Madan, "Loki" to his friends, and his wife; he had until recently, headed Delhi University's Institute of Economic Growth. I also try to see my old friends there, and Sylvia visits with me if her work schedule permits. P.N. and Sheila Dhar, after his retirement as U.N. Undersecretary, returned to Delhi, where she died, and he still lives there. Sunitha Raju, my research assistant in Hyderabad in 1984, moved to Delhi to work there and later married and lives there. Prakash Tandon lived there for many years until he left to live with his son in Pune before he died. Sukhamoy and Lalita Chakravarty were there at Delhi University, and we always met until he died some years back. Lalita has moved to another part of the city, and we always try to see her when we are there.

Sylvia's research has focused on the religious and legal position of Muslim women in India. She has been particularly interested in marriage and divorce issues. She has interviewed many wives and husbands, both divorced and married, to discuss this, and lawyers involved in such cases, as well as examined court records when available. She has also talked with local Muslim religious figures on those issues when they are willing to be interviewed. In her work she has become friends with different Muslim families, and met one woman, Zakira Ghouse, a widow with whom she became a close friend. Zakira, who lived in Madras with her daughter and son-in-law in a family home, was an elderly woman from a leading Hyderabad Muslim family. She had been unusual when she was young in that she received a college education and taught at a woman's college in the state; she was also married and had children. Now that is not unusual, but it had been very much so earlier. She wrote her autobiography in Urdu, the local language, and Sylvia is having it translated into English in hope of publishing it. We have met Zakira's family members on our stays in Madras. Zakira died recently, but Sylvia always sees them when she is in South India. Some of her younger family now work and live in the United States and Canada, and we have seen them here. Sylvia is "auntie" to them, and I am "uncle," though they know I am Jewish. This makes me feel very good, and gives me a sense of the tolerance of Muslims. In the 2004 summer we were invited to a family wedding in Canada. Sylvia was able to go, but I couldn't for my own family reasons. She had a very enjoyable time and she was told how much Uncle George was missed.

In addition to visits to India for that research Sylvia has been invited to spend some time at the French Institute of Indian Studies in Pondicherry to attend conferences and to discuss ongoing research by French scholars there. I have gone with her and met various scholars there. The one I got to know best is Lorraine Kennedy, an economist from the United States who received her Ph.D. from the Sorbonne, now lives in France with her husband and child, teaches there and has worked in India. She has done interesting work on village enterprises in South India. I have benefited from her work, and Sylvia and I are very glad to have met her and her husband socially as well. Pondicherry is an interesting place to visit for other reasons as well. One of the best Indian handicraft centers that I know is in the state, and there are some very attractive nature areas. Alice Thorner is a colleague and friend of many of the leading French scholars on India. When we are in Paris, we often meet several of them at Alice's home where we may be staying or somewhere else in the city as their guests.

Before going on further about myself and Sylvia, I want to catch up with Mark's life and Sylvia's children during our years in Wisconsin and overseas research, and with my own family on the east coast. For our children this was a period of starting their careers and getting on; for my family of my generation there were deaths and changes.

Mark graduated from Law School in the early 1980's. He decided to become an officer in the Army's Legal Department in which he served for his years of service. He worked in U.S. locations and also for some years with American troops stationed in Korea and briefly in several other Asian countries. When we were in China in 1986-1987, he was in Korea, but he could not get leave to visit us in China, and we weren't able to get to Korea. When his military service ended, he joined a law firm in Chicago for a few years. It was a large firm, and he didn't find his law work there very interesting. He and a colleague, Mike Holzman, then set up their own small law firm outside of Milwaukee, while Sylvia and I were still in Lake Geneva. From what he tells me they have done well and do a great deal of public defender work that Mark enjoys professionally. Mike also does other types of legal work, and he was in fact our lawyer when we sold the Lake Geneva house.

Mark met Kymberlee, his future wife, in about 1995. They hit it off and were married in 1996. It was a large and very happy wedding outside of Milwaukee. We of course were there and participated actively, as did Kusum, Mark's mother, though we sat separately. Sylvia's four children and Arna's son, Dallas, were also there and had a good time. We had naturally met Kitt Egan, Kymberlee's mother, well before the marriage and became good friends seeing each other often since, and we met Kymberlee's brothers and sisters then. When we are in Chicago, we see Mark and Kymberlee about once a month in Milwaukee or Chicago. Kymberlee was working in theatre before her wedding, and she enjoys both theatre and art, which we do also. They now have two children, Quinn eight and Kaylee five. It's a great pleasure to watch them grow. Kymberlee has been fully occupied raising them in their pre-school years. Mark is with them at home when he is not in court. They have a very nice house outside of Milwaukee in a pleasant green area, and close enough to the city to enjoy that as well. I just heard, while writing this chapter, that Kitt unexpectedly died. It was a great shock for Sylvia and me. She had lived near her children, and they very much enjoyed being with her and traveling with her in Europe as well as the U.S. Kitt had a senior post with an agency that reviews applicants for college admissions in the U.S. which kept her very busy during the college application period – she made a major contribution to that work. Her death is a great personal loss for us, as well as her children.

Of Sylvia's children Sanjaya lives nearest to us in Chicago today. He works as a computer technician out of Eastman Kodak's Chicago office and lives in Chicago's Oak Park suburb where he has a very pleasant house. We see him often in the city, and he has been most helpful in our frequent moves within Chicago and to and from there in the summer and whenever Sylvia's computers have a problem. He is not married and is a vegetarian. He enjoys movies and rock music, and his hobby is automobiles. It is always great to see him.

Arna now works and lives in and near San Diego where she is a partner in the accounting firm she has been associated with for many years. We see her regularly every summer when she visits us in Falmouth, and she often visits in Chicago. We go out to San Diego to spend a holiday with her at least every other year. Dallas, now twenty-two, lives in her house, but with his own life with his auto-repair work, and attendance in a pre-engineering academic program. Arna's companion for the past ten years, Robby O'Hare, an electrical engineer living in Los Angeles, comes to San Diego weekends or she goes up there, and he usually comes with Arna to Falmouth in the summer, and we see him whenever we are in San Diego. Arna is a great companion, and she is a most caring daughter. She handles all our tax problems and her advice on Sylvia's financial and related questions is always most useful. Robby is a very pleasant companion when he is with us, and very helpful on Falmouth house problems. Dallas has spent many summers with us in Bristol and Falmouth while he was growing up. He learned to sail here and often sails on some boat in a race when there is one in Falmouth. He is a great grandson, most helpful around the house when here and as a person for the sheer pleasure of being with him.

Sunita is Sylvia's one married child until now. She is the most socially and intellectually oriented. In California where she lived in Berkeley in the 1970's she was very supportive of various reform movements there and in Central America. After completing her undergraduate work, she went to Princeton to get her doctorate in Math. While there she met David Claman, a fellow graduate student in the Music Department. They developed a close relationship and were married in 1998 in New York City Hall shortly before they went to India on an AIIS grant; we were there that same year on Sylvia's research grant. We had a big wedding party in the summer in Falmouth after we all returned. They had lived in Princeton while studying, then in India for their time there, and then in Colorado where they were both teaching before moving to Worcester, Massachusetts. After David got his Ph.D. from Princeton, he was appointed Assistant Professor in Music at Holy Cross in Worcester. They have an apartment there where they live during the academic year when they are not on leave. They have also lived in New York City occasionally. David is a composer whose work has been played by leading orchestras in the country. Sunita had been teaching math at Worcester Technical Institute near Holy Cross. She has also taken up ceramics as a major interest and has been making lovely pottery of her own design. She has studio facilities for ceramics and works there regularly. This past summer we used one of their cars in Falmouth, and they are most helpful around the house whenever they are here. When we meet, they are most enjoyable company with their interest in international affairs and social issues, as well as their pleasure in music, art and theatre. It's great to talk to them and to go with them to concerts, though I think we like to listen to Baroque music and Mozart more than they do today. I may agree with them somewhat less on some specific social issues than Sylvia does, but we generally see eye to eye.

Sylvia's youngest son, Jai, is a musician who has been living in southern California for many years until very recently. He is a rock and reggae performer with many different groups on the guitar and electric instruments which he plays. When we are in California, we enjoy going to hear him. We are probably the oldest people there, but it is a pleasure to watch the young dancers dancing to the music and the listening audiences, and sometimes we've danced when we've been carried away by the rhythms. Since Jai is very busy and on the move, we see less of him than our other children. At one time he had a Filipina companion whom I liked a lot – she reminded me of friends I had in Manila – but they separated in the past few years. He recently moved to Idaho to work for an entertainment company in Boise. That may be an excuse for a railroad trip from Chicago to the west coast. I only had one such trip when I was in the army in 1943, and I still remember how attractive Idaho was then. In any case we hope we will be in more frequent touch with him in his new work since it is so enjoyable to be with him. We saw all of Sylvia's children at the very moving Memorial Service of her sister, Judy, in January 2005 in Massachusetts.

There have been many changes in my family with whom I was raised. Walter had died in 1987 when I was in China. My brother Paul also died of cancer ten years ago. He was a year older than I and while I was growing up in Bridgeport we were very close. He had married Gladys, my step-niece, in 1944 while serving in the Air Force. We had much in common though his interest and career was in engineering rather than the social fields. I was very close to him and Gladys after their marriage. His death was a great blow, and I have tried to give Gladys whatever support I can after his death. I see her every summer and talk to her regularly when in the U.S. It has not been easy for her. We often see her younger daughter, Laurie, a good musician, and her son-in-law, Harold, with their family who live in Stratford, Connecticut, not far from her, who are very helpful to her. Her older daughter, Debby, an artist, and her husband, Randy, live near Rochester, New York, and we have visited with them several times in travel to or from Chicago.

My sisters Helen and Gert are still wonderful to talk to and see. Helen is now ninety-three and still lives in the house she and Sam lived in before he died some years back in his nineties. He had been a very close friend and with Helen had watched over Helen's and my mothers, who lived in the house next door. He was a very able lawyer, a state legislator in Connecticut and very active in the state and city Democratic Party. He knew politics at all levels, and it was most interesting to be with him as well as to enjoy joint pleasures. He had great taste in art and collected paintings of contemporary artists in Connecticut and New York. I tried to see Helen and Sam whenever I was near Bridgeport of course. For many years he and Helen went to Chatauqua in New York state for the summer season there. They rented an apartment there and went to the lectures, concerts, plays and art shows, as well as the nearby lake shore, enjoying themselves very much. Sylvia and I would visit them there driving from Chicago to Bristol or Falmouth, if that were possible, and that was always enjoyable. His death was also a great personal loss. Helen showed great courage after he died, and has shown remarkable strength and capacity to enjoy life since. She is a model for me in her continued wide range of interest in reading, gardening, New York culture, current events and politics. I hope I'll be the same when I'm her age. Her son, Andy, and his wife, Marcia, live nearby and that is very helpful; her daughter Judy comes down from the Boston district often and son Richard from near New York. It is great she can stay in the house; she does not want to go to a retirement home, which I fully appreciate. When we visit Bridgeport, we usually stay with Andy and Marcia, since we don't want to add any work for Helen, but she always wants to make a meal for us at home. I talk to her at least once a week when I'm in the U.S.

My younger sister, Gert, lives in Florida. I talk to her regularly, and she is in quite good health. She enjoys Florida with two of her daughters and their husbands and children living fairly near. Her older daughter, Lea, a doctor, lives near New York and Gert stays with her when she is in the north. Gert comes with Lea to Bridgeport every summer. When they do, Sylvia and I come down from Falmouth to meet them in or near Bridgeport. We've had family lunches together with them and Helen and Gladys when that is possible, and I always enjoy those. It is so good to see them.

Walter's youngest son, Johnny, who was close to me, died at age forty-seven. That was a real shock and a personal loss. Robert, Walter's oldest son, and his wife, Diane, live in Boston, and we see each other every summer, and as I mentioned, Daniel, his middle son, and his wife, Leslie, live near Washington, and his son, Zachary, now in Chicago studying.

Whenever we come to Bridgeport to see Helen, we usually see Andy and Marcia in Bridgeport, or at their son's place near Cape Cod. Andy, a lawyer, headed Bridgeport's public defender office for many years until he retired. It's a coincidence that he and Mark were in the same area of law, but in two different states. We see Judy and Al in the summer every year, and talk to Richard and Rise – though we have not met very often. The family occasions I or we may meet all of them are celebrations such as the marriages of their children, Bar or Bat-Mitzvahs of their grandchildren, or the sadder occasions of funerals. I am glad when we celebrate together.

Until now I have written of my family on my mother's side, in which I was raised as a child, and on Sylvia's side, but not of my step-father's side, except for Gladys, my step-niece. She had married Paul and, like Helen and Gert, has been a sister to me. Eva, my step-sister whom I was closest to, died some years back, and Harry, her husband, had died before her. I have been in contact quite regularly with their son, Arthur, and his wife, Althea. He had worked for a management firm for many years before retiring recently, and Althea taught in a New York state school. Their daughter, Felice, who works in New York City, was married to John Smith in the summer of 2003 at a large wedding in Connecticut, and it was a pleasure to celebrate with them, and see again family members whom I had not seen or heard from for many years. Felice and John recently had their first child.

Barbara Ledgin is the only other member of my step-father's family that I am in touch with fairly regularly, by phone if not in person. She is the daughter of my oldest step-brother, Max, who died many years ago. Barbara has married, has several children and now lives in a New York suburb. She travels quite a bit, visiting Spain often, and I have not seen her since Felice's wedding. Her daughter, Stephanie, is in theatre, lives in New Jersey with her husband, and we exchange cards every year. Stephanie has just published a book on Bluegrass music.

Before ending this family chapter, I want to write of another cousin with whom I was close before he died several years back. Muni Yavnieli lived in Israel with his wife, Dvora, and their son, Yuval. Muni's parents had gone to Israel from Russia before the First World War, at about the time my Aunt Esther had come to the United States – he was related to my mother's and aunt's family. He was a Zionist and settled in a kibbutz (a farm cooperative) there. Muni was about my age, and during the Second World War he fought with an Israeli military unit fighting with the British against German attacks in the Mid-East, and later as insurgents against British rule in Israel and for an independent state there. He met his wife then – she was also associated with the insurgency movement.

I had not known of them until the 1960's or later. If I remember rightly, I think Walter had met them first on a visit to Israel. Somewhat later their son, Yuval, came to the United States for some study and visited with us for some days in the Boston area. On one of my later trips to Asia in the 1970's I went to Israel for the first time. I stayed with Muni and Dvora, then living in Beer Sheba, where Muni was an engineer in a factory there. It was a fascinating trip. Muni took me to Jerusalem to visit the Wailing Wall and other Holy areas and to the

Hebrew University, to northern Israel to Hebron and the Lebanese border, and east to the Dead Sea and Jordan. We swam in the Dead Sea; floating was easy. In Jerusalem too we walked through some of the Muslim areas of the city, giving me a sense of another society. With my experience in Asia I had the sense of Israel having a comparatively developed economy, more so than many of Asia's economies in which I had worked.

After that visit, I remained in regular contact with Muni and Dvora, and visited again for a week in 1994 after my month in Egypt. At that time Muni had retired from his work in Beer Sheba, and he and Dvora were living in Raanana, a town near Tel Aviv. This was an upper income area of the country, and I stayed in their apartment there. It was a very pleasant visit, I traveled some with them to visit Yuval and his family in Tel Aviv, where Yuval practiced law, to the beach near that city for swimming, to Hebron and to Jerusalem. The country was peaceful, and we traveled freely and safely.

Muni, who of course knew far more than I did of Israel's political situation, was not hopeful of future Israeli relations with its neighbors and with Arafat. He believed Israel's military strength was its main safeguard against Arab threats to its survival. Yuval, who had served duty in the Israeli army as is required of all Israeli youth, was then less militant than his father. I remember he thought peaceful relations were possible with the Arabs and wanted the Israeli government to pursue a peaceful settlement in Israel itself, and with its neighbors. I don't know his present opinion since I lost touch with him after Muni died.

I was very glad to spend time with Muni and Dvora, to see Yuval again and meet his wife and children. It turned out to be my last chance to do so. Muni died some years after, and it has been hard to reach Dvora since then. His death is a real personal loss; he and Dvora were very close friends. I have heard that Yuval has separated from his family, and I'm told he is not in touch with them. I know I've lost touch completely with him, which I very much regret.

I am glad Israel exists. I was not a Zionist before the Second World War, and I am not a religious Jew since I am not a believer in the Jewish, or any other, God. But after what I saw and heard of the Holocaust with its persecution and killing of millions of Jews in Hitler's Germany and Europe during the Second World War, I believe there is a need for a nation in which Jews are safe. That was the reason for the establishment of independent Israel in which Jews from all over the world are safe. I fully support that state, but I also believe it is essential for the future of the state that it establish a peaceful and stable relationship with the Muslim countries on all sides of Israel. Furthermore, the Arab people within Israel must retain the full rights they have as citizens of a democracy. I also believe for a peaceful Israel-Arab long-term relationship, it is very important that a stable, independent Palestine state be established. I think Muslim fundamentalism is a threat to those goals, but I also think the killing of Prime Minister Rabin by a fundamentalist Jewish assassin because of his peaceful policies was a disaster.

I think religious fundamentalism in every religion today is one of the greatest present threats to democracy and to world peace. The same holds true for racial fundamentalism. Both must be fought in the United States and anywhere else in the world. Their consequences in Africa, the Middle East and Eastern Europe have been disastrous and murderous. The results of religious fundamentalism in the South Asian countries I know have also been murderous and threatening. Fighting those fundamentalisms and dealing with their consequences is a major task of the United Nations today, for which American support is vital. As part of that fight, I do not believe that the U.S. should support any fundamentalist movements in any country for short-term policy purposes, as it has in the past. We should now have learned that its long-term consequences can be disastrous, as it was in Afghanistan, with the Taliban and Al Qaeda. Within our country itself religious and racial intolerance must be fought as a major social priority.

I have gotten away from my family relations, on which this chapter focuses, but I thought I might mention this important issue as I write of my cousins in Israel. I am an American citizen of a Jewish ethnic upbringing, and I think Israel's future is important. I also feel that American's role is vital today in making the world a livable place for all of the world's people, where we can live together peacefully, freely, and under improving conditions of life. It has gradually occurred in a united, free United States since the Civil War and in Western Europe since 1945. It can be achieved in the other countries of the world. For this we must work with and through the United Nations with other countries. We cannot impose our own rules which may not be directly relevant in other societies, but we should seek that end cooperatively.

CHAPTER XIII

My Life in my Seventies and Eighties Until Today

T HIS IS MY last chapter. I have worked, written another book before this one, made a new and close friend and lived a full and pleasurable life with Sylvia, and our children and grandchildren, and my family members and niece and nephews.

The book was published in 1996 by Avebury Press. Entitled *Economic Development in Asia*, it is a collection of many of my articles going back to my first one. I thought this volume would show the growth of my thinking in the field of economic development from an institutional and historical framework. It should be useful for anyone looking at some of the development problems of the late 20th century, and may be of value not only for economists, but also for policy analysis with respect to Asia's economic future. There may have been one or two reviews – I don't remember any now. It's still in print – I've been able to order copies for friends.

I did one very interesting research project. A friend of mine, Tom Timberg, had done major work on the Indian economy. He knows my work on India well. He is on the staff of Robert Nathan Associates, a major consulting firm in the Washington area, that has done consultancy work for USAID in developing countries. One of its contracts was with the Egyptian government in 1994 to advise on its economic reform program to reduce controls and stimulate private domestic industry. Tom, who knew of my work on India and China, asked me to be a member of that advisory group. We would go to Egypt for about a month to talk to Egyptian officials and private businessmen, to review what had been happening on the reform program and recommend changes and further actions. I accepted Tom's offer – it was a challenge and an opportunity. I had never worked in Egypt before, and I hoped to learn about the country and its economy. As a side benefit, I hoped to see one of the great countries of world civilization that I had never spent any time in before, apart from a Suez Canal trip from India.

My month there was a most interesting one, even though there had been, shortly before, a period of terrorist attacks in the country. I and my two colleagues lived in Cairo with office space in an Egyptian government building. An Egyptian Economics Professor, Mahmoud Hosny, was associated with our research, providing contacts, advice and assistance. We met various government officials in Economic ministries, leading Egyptian businessmen and some foreign investors and knowledgeable academics. We also visited different factories and some other nearby areas of the country to see what was happening outside of Cairo. We then wrote a report for the Egyptian government. I didn't keep up with events after that to know if it had any policy effect, but apart from that it was most interesting.

Cairo was for me a most unusual city. Its location on the Nile is very attractive and our hotel was near the river. A walk along it before the day became too hot, was very enjoyable. It was a very crowded city and very busy with a fascinating market area. In those markets bargaining was the center of buying anything. One of my colleagues, who had spent much time in Cairo in his career, loved the bargaining and I thought he went to the market for that pleasure, as much as for the very attractive products he bought. The Cairo Museum is one of the world's greatest. Its collection of sculpture and other art from the great periods of Egyptian history is unsurpassed. A visit there was most exciting and satisfying. I have told friends since then, only half joking, that if I had visited that museum when I was going to college, I would have become an archeologist of Egyptian history instead of an economist. (One of Chicago's charms is the University of Chicago's Oriental Institute with its great collection of Egyptian art.)

Outside of Cairo are some of the great Egyptian Pyramids, the Giza Pyramids and the Sphinx among others, great monuments. I visited those, but we did not have time to go to the Southern pyramids and temples because of pressure of our work. It was also not a good time to travel there because of the terrorism, so I missed those, which I very much regret.

Sylvia and I had good friends in Cairo. T.J. Anderson's son and his wife were teaching at the American University there, and they introduced me to Egyptian faculty who were very knowledgeable of the city and country. Mahmoud couldn't have been more helpful both as an associate in our work and as a friend. I met his family members in the city in that month. Through friends I went to some Egyptian restaurants for excellent food, and to various musical and theatrical events in the city which I enjoyed very much.

One of my colleagues on the consulting group was Harold Lubell. I had first known Harold from Bard College where he had been one of Adolf Sturmthal's students before I taught there, and we met later, when I taught there, when he visited Adolf. Then we had seen each other occasionally after that. He had worked for the U.S. government and international aid agencies in the Middle East including Egypt and knew it well. He was also a skilled cellist and had played in a Cairo orchestra while living there, and knew the city and culture well. He now lives in Paris and is an artist, and I see him when I go to Paris. Renewing our friendship was a great personal gain of that work.

I remain in touch with Tom Timberg, whom I try to see when I'm in Washington, though he is out of the U.S. often for his work with Robert Nathan. I've already written about my trip to Israel for a week after I had gone to Cairo. I mentioned to Muni that I thought the Egyptians I met had been personally friendly though they knew I was

Jewish and going to Israel. I added that I had a general impression of friendliness toward Israel on a more official level and in the newspapers, but he was skeptical as to how deep that was.

The third result from my work as an economist in the 1990's and since is my meeting Eberhard Reusse, a German economist. I had not known him before then, but he knew that I was the Book Editor of EDCC. He had worked for many years with the United Nations Food and Agricultural Organization (FAO) as an advisor on agricultural development in Asia and Africa, working and living in several Asian and many Sub-Saharan countries. On the basis of that experience he had written a book on rural development issues at the village level, in it discussing the contributions of foreign advisory agencies, both government and non-government. The book was in English, published by a German publisher – it was his Ph.D. thesis in Economics after he decided to get that degree. He sent it to me for review in EDCC and for my suggestions for possible publication in the United States. I read it with a great deal of interest, and felt it made a major contribution to thinking in the Economic Development field. It stressed the importance of the local cultures and social conditions in both making and implementing policies and providing assistance, financial and technical, for rural development. Terry Neale, Kusum Nair and Don Kanel had stressed this in their work on India many years ago, but I had not seen it argued on a worldwide basis. I suggested to Geoff Huck that the University of Chicago Press publish it, and that was done after the usual readings and some editorial revision. Eberhard was very appreciative of my help on this. It turned out that his daughter and son-in-law and family were living near Chicago, and Eberhard visits them at least once a year. As a result Sylvia and I see him in Chicago just about every year. In 2001 we had gone to their rented summer place in Switzerland for about a week, during which Sylvia and I went for a day in Salzburg, Austria, my first time there. He invited us to visit him and his wife, Ruth, in Dortmund, Germany, and we had a very pleasant few days there in 2003.

I will write about Eberhard at some length. He and Ruth are my first German friends who have been born and lived there from the period of Hitler. I have known many refugees from Hitler's Germany,

Lore Segal best, and many others; Elfriede Blanco-Gonzalez had been born in wartime Germany in what became East Germany after the war. Elfriede was able to come to the U.S. to study at Chicago where she met Manuel. I had been in the American army in Germany during the war and had met some local Germans in passing, but I certainly knew none. After the War, I had not wanted to go back to Germany. That was the country in which the Jews had been annihilated. I wondered when I met a non-Jewish German of my age in the course of my later career what he or she had done during Hitler's rule, but I did not feel I could ask. I knew of Germany's and Austria's great contribution to European art and literature, and the great architecture from centuries back to the modern Bauhaus before Hitler. This had made the rule of Hitler even more of a shock; I have been very much interested in the history of Hitler's rise and rule, but I did not want to go to Germany. (Sylvia spent her Cornell junior year abroad in 1953 in Munich.) Eberhard is the first German citizen I have gotten to know well, whom I have visited in Germany since the War. I am very glad I met him and Ruth. They are most hospitable. I enjoy exchanging ideas with them both on general political and social issues in Europe and America, and on development questions in the countries we have lived and worked in. Eberhard is interested in the Jews in the United States and asks me about that (I'm not very knowledgeable), and I ask him about German Jews today. He has been my own main contact to today's Germany.

Sylvia has her own German friends. She had first spent a year there in 1953. More recently, after our marriage we had visited Germany together before I met Eberhard. There are several anthropological centers in Germany where research on India is being done. She has been invited to attend meetings and give talks at universities in Berlin, Heidelberg and Cologne in recent years, and she recently went to Munich on the 50th anniversary of her junior year abroad. I was with her on those occasions. Her closest German anthropologist friend is Helena Basu at the Freie University in Berlin with whom we have stayed in Berlin, and who has visited with us in Chicago. We freely discuss intellectual, social and political issues in Germany, America and Asia with her and other friends.

I had no sense of the Nazi heritage in the social and intellectual events I've participated in. Heidelberg and Cologne are beautiful cities, with their old palaces and churches. Berlin has been rebuilt after the War and more recently since the unification of West and East Germany and Berlin. Munich has also been rebuilt since my few days there in the army in 1945. Both cities are very attractive and have some of the world's greatest art museums, with collections from medieval to contemporary art.

Apart from Germany's great cultural attractions, I wanted to see the Holocaust Museum in Berlin. This was at Wahnsee in the building where the Nazi leaders made the decision to move ahead toward the Annihilation of the Jews. In going there, seeing the documents and photographs gave me a sense of the immediate annihilation events that I had not had in the U.S. Holocaust Museum. I was glad to see in the Wahnsee Center that school classes were also there, showing that German children were being taught about the Holocaust. While in Munich, we went to the Dachau Concentration Camp outside Munich, which has been restored as a Holocaust Museum. This gave an actual sense of what the Jews, and others such as Gypsies and East Europeans, had undergone in the actual quarters in which they lived, and the death chambers in which they were killed. In Berlin in 2003 we visited the old Jewish neighborhood and the synagogue, which was being rebuilt on an earlier visit, and which was finished later. In some districts of the city houses which had once belonged to Jews were marked with the names of the former inhabitants, and plaques were placed on sidewalks with names of people who had been sent to camps.

Those days in Germany, and especially the visit to Dachau, also gave me a sense of what might have happened to me if my mother had not come with me to the United States in 1923. While I was not German, if we had stayed in the Soviet Union I might have been killed by German invaders in White Russia, as my grandfather had been, or near Leningrad during the German siege of the city. Or I might have been sent to a Russian concentration camp during Stalin's rule for some reason or other, including being a Jew. Hitler was defeated, overthrown by American, English, and Russian troops in a war in which I was in the American army. I am proud I was, that I did help to overthrow Hitler and am glad that I could visit a friendly and alive Germany fifty years after.

One of my closest friends, Heinz Arndt, who died in the past few years, was another refugee from Germany, before coming to England and then Australia. Sylvia and I visited him and his wife, Ruth, in Australia, where they lived in Canberra after he retired as Economics Professor at the Australian National University. We had known each other well for over forty years from the work we each were doing in Asia. Our paths had crossed often there, he had visited us in Chicago, and he was the best correspondent I have known. Fortunately we were able to come to Australia to visit with him and Ruth, whom I had not met, before they died. That trip in 2000 was triggered by John and Virginia's suggestion that we join them to visit Dorothy Grover, an old and mutual friend of ours who had headed the UIC Philosophy Department who returned to her home country, New Zealand, after she retired. She had been Irv Thalberg's friend and colleague, and I had known her well at UIC myself. We had never been to New Zealand and heard it is a beautiful country. Dorothy lives near Christ Church on the South Island, and that island is as beautiful as its reputation – its lakes and mountains are spectacular, and we had a lovely cruise on the ocean. We also saw some of the Maori art and a rebuilt village near Auckland in the north, and that was enjoyable.

En route to New Zealand we stopped in Canberra with Heinz and Ruth. We were very glad we did – it was a great pleasure to meet Ruth, and, like always, to spend time with Heinz, to exchange ideas and to sightsee around Canberra with them. In retrospect our visit was even more fortunate in its timing. Ruth died within a year after our visit. Heinz died several years later from hitting a tree on the ANU campus while driving his car and suffering a stroke. He was one of my closest friends among economists and a great correspondent, and I miss him greatly. This makes our visit with them one I am especially glad I could make. Otherwise I would never have met Ruth, seen them at home or seen him again. On this visit we also spent several days in Sydney as guests of their daughter, Bettina, and her husband, Warren. Sydney is a city I like – it reminds me of San Francisco. I had been there once before, and it has a lovely theatre and museum and overview of the ocean. Bettina and Warren were very hospitable. We remained in touch with them until after Heinz's death, but seem to have lost contact in the past year or so.

Another couple I met only in 2003 whom I am glad to know are Alex and Ella Gorlov, who live near us in Falmouth. They are in their late sixties now, and are fairly recent immigrants from the Soviet Union, leaving there during Brezhnev's rule. He had been an engineer at an important Russian research institution. Ella had also been a scientist. He is now an Emeritus Professor at Northeastern University in Boston in that field. They had known Alexander Solzhenitsin somewhat before Solzhenitsin had been forced into exile. Alex Gorlov's story of the effects of a visit to Solzhenitsin's house when Solzhenitsin was not there upon his and his wife's life and career in Russia, and their decision to leave that country is fascinating. They are also Jewish, which had affected their careers even apart from his acquaintance with Solzhenitsin. They were subject to constant surveillance as an acquaintance of Solzhenitsin, and limits were placed on his career as a scientist because of that and of being a Jew. His published autobiography, *Incident at a Summer House*, which he wrote in Europe after he left Russia, and is available in English, is the best book I know of what it must have been like to have been a scholar or scientist, Jewish or not, in Russia during the Communist dictatorship. It gave me a picture of what my life might have been in the Soviet Union if my mother had not brought me to the United States, and I had grown up there and survived the Second World War and Stalin's rule.

Since the year 2000 when I reached 80, with great celebration, I have accompanied Sylvia to India on her research work. We were en route there on her AIIS grant on September 11, 2001, when terrorists attacked the World Trade Center in New York City and the Pentagon. We were driving from the Barcelona airport to our hotel when we heard of the attacks. Our taxi driver, speaking in Spanish, asked us if we heard of them. We thought he was speaking of a TV show, when he told us we could see it on TV. We did turn the TV on in our room, and we realized it was real – it was like watching another Pearl Harbor. We wondered whether we should go on to India. Sylvia contacted the AIIS offices in Chicago and India, and we read the U.S. State Department warnings. From what we heard from AIIS and friends in India we decided to go ahead, and we did. The few days in Barcelona were very interesting and pleasant. We had just passed through the city on our first visit to Spain, but then our sense was of a big overgrown city. On this trip we visited parks in the city, the Picasso and other museums and, what I was especially struck by, Gaudi's architectural works. I think he is one of the greatest of modern architects. The cathedral he designed, unfortunately still incomplete, is a spectacular entree to the city, and the house and gardens he designed, now a museum and park, are very enjoyable.

On that trip after we left Barcelona we visited Eberhard in Switzerland. While the weather was rainy, I had never been in that part of Switzerland before and during our stay there we went to Salzburg for a day; it was full of other tourists. I would have liked to have gone to Vienna, where I have never been, but that was too far away. From there we returned to London for our flight to India.

Sylvia's research was in Hyderabad, where we knew many people and had good friends from past work and years lived there. As I mentioned, it is a city with a Muslim history and a large Muslim population, and we wondered after 9/11 if Sylvia's work on Muslim women would go smoothly. In fact it did, and she received all she wanted for her work from Muslim friends, lawyers and religious figures. We also were struck by the friendly Muslim-Hindu relations in the city after 9/11. While there were some demonstrations of both militant Muslims and Hindus, they were peaceful demonstrations and there were no religious conflicts during our time there. One of the side pleasures of that time was our visit to Hampi, about 12 hours from Hyderabad, that had been the capital of the early Jayanagar Empire of that section of India. While many of the palaces and temples had been destroyed over time, archeologists have recovered many of them and they are being rebuilt. It is a beautiful historical complex, and I like the architectural style of the period very much. The countryside around Hampi is also very attractive, so the entire few days there were both interesting and enjoyable.

In Hyderabad we saw our good friends Geeta Gouri and Rajan, the Somayajulus and the Mahender Reddys, and I gave one or two talks. We visited Madras for Sylvia's work, and while there spent time with the Vaidyanathans and Kuriens and at the MIDS where I met other friends. I also visited Bangalore to be with Krishnaswamy and Madhura. While Sylvia was working in the south, I went to Bombay where I spent several days at the Indira Gandhi Institute of Development Research, where I was invited by my old friend Professor R. Radhakrishna, who now headed it. I gave several talks there on technological change and industrial growth and encouraged research on India's policy in that area. I of course met old friends in Bombay with their families. These included the Sabavalas, Sandesaras, Pendses, Saroj Hazari and her children and Carmen Kagal. I also went to Calcutta for several days to see Harendra Mazumdar and Ashok and Gouri Mitra; in Delhi we saw again Prakash Tandon, P.N. Dhar, Lalita Chakravarty, Sunitha Raju and Isher Ahluwalia. Thus that trip made it possible for me not only to get a sense of India, but, even more pleasurable, to see old friends, many of whom I had not seen for years.

Sylvia and I have gone on several trips with Virginia and John in the past ten years. As I mentioned, Virginia has both great taste in travel, and is an excellent trip arranger. We have gone to Mexico with them three times. Those were my first trips there, and the first time I've ever been south of the Rio Grande. I've had Latino students, I had hired a Mexican economist, José Alberro, for UIC when I was Department Head, and I had met various South American economists during my work with international agencies, but I had never gone there. On these trips with Virginia and John we were tourists. Our first visit was to San Miguel de Allende, the town in which the Mexican revolution against Spain had begun. Limits have been set on its development to prevent loss of its character, and it retains a Spanish historical character and is located in an attractive region. There were older churches and buildings we enjoyed visiting. Many Mexican artists lived in or near it. It was an upscale town that attracted retired Americans, so it could not be considered a typical city in that respect, but we had a very pleasant week there. I was also able to visit a local textile factory on a guided tour and could ask some questions about the work in it. During those two weeks, we also drove to Guanajuato, a silver mining town near San Miguel in which Diego Rivera was born and lived as a boy. His family home is now a museum devoted to his early work. I enjoyed that very much. I had known his work for many years and liked it, but he was not one of my favorite artists. His work that I knew was too monumental and political for my taste in art. In the museum there were very many of his earlier, smaller paintings and prints, and these I liked very much. I have since gone to shows of his work in Chicago and elsewhere when I can. I also saw more of the work of his wife, Frida Kahlo, that I also like very much and try to see. In fact I have developed a broader taste for contemporary Mexican art which is some of the best world art I know.

Our second trip to Mexico was to Puerto Vallarta on the northern Baja California Peninsula, not far from the American border. That town has really become a tourist center, and I had little sense of Mexico. We went swimming off the beach, and we took a pleasant boat trip along the coast, on which we saw some fishing villages that didn't seem touristy.

Our third, most recent trip was to Todas Santos in the southern area of the Baja California Peninsula. The home we stayed in had a lovely location with the ocean very near, and was surrounded by rural country. We enjoyed that very much. I want to go back to Mexico again to see the Aztec country – I have admired the Aztec sculpture and other work of that civilization that I have seen pictures of, and I hope to see them in real life. I have also never been to Mexico City, which I am told is an overwhelming city. I want to see it both for itself and as a development economist to get a sense of how Mexico has grown economically.

We have most recently gone to Crete in Greece with Virginia and John. That is one of the most beautiful places that I have ever visited, and it combines its beauty with the remains of classical Greek civilization. Thus from my friendship with Virginia and John I've been able to see parts of the world I had neither seen before nor would probably ever have seen. That has been a very enjoyable part of that friendship with our closest friends in Chicago at whose apartment we celebrated Sylvia's 70th birthday.

This concludes my autobiography. I wanted to write it now. In the past year many close friends and former colleagues have died, and I have become conscious of death in a stronger sense than ever before, since I left the army – and I wanted to write my record. I have had a full life and that life was made possible by my mother's immigration to the United States and the opportunities I had here. I want other American children, and children in other countries of the world, to have similar opportunities. That is why I support the free international migration of people regarding it as an international benefit of globalization. I hope that by my work as a development economist in the United States and in many developing countries of Asia and as a teacher in this country and others, I contributed to making a better life both for my fellow Americans and people overseas. I believe many other current immigrants to this country are contributing greatly to America's well-being now, as they have done in the past, and that supports my belief that free immigration into America from all the world's countries is a national benefit. There may be costs, but these are much less than the benefits, and they can be reduced or eliminated by intelligent policy actions.

I want to add one final paragraph on my career as an economist. I am glad that I became one when I did. With my socialist family background, broad institutional and historical education in economics, and the public policy approach of economists writing and working in the years of Franklin Roosevelt and The New Deal, including those who taught me, I wanted to, and felt I could, make a contribution to a better world by practicing economics. I think I have done that. I have the sense that economics has become much narrower in approach, far more mathematical in its method, and less open-minded with respect to policy today than it was sixty years ago when I studied it. I think that is a real loss, and I very much hope that its broad character and flexibility returns to what it had been. I am very glad I was an economist and could do what I have done, but I'm not sure that practicing what economics has become today would give me, personally, and society, the same satisfactions and benefits in the future as it gave in the past.

APPENDIX

List of George Rosen's Economic Books

Industrial Change in India (1958)

Some Aspects of Industrial Finance in India (1962)

Democracy and Economic Change in India (1966-67)

Peasant Society in a Changing Economy (1975)

Decision – Making Chicago Style: The Genesis of a University of Illinois Campus (1980)

Western Economists and Eastern Societies (1985)

Industrial Change in India, 1970-2000 (1988)

Contrasting Styles of Industrial Reform: China and India in the 1980s (1992)

Economic Development in Asia (1996)